The Original
Tuxedo Jazz Band

The Original Tuxedo Jazz Band

More than a Century of a New Orleans Icon

Sally Newhart

Charleston H London
THE
History
PRESS

Published by The History Press
Charleston, SC 29403
www.historypress.net

Copyright © 2013 by Sally Newhart
All rights reserved

Back cover, bottom left: Waldren "Frog" Joseph at Dixieland Hall, 1964.
Courtesy of the Hogan Jazz Archive, Tulane.

First published 2013

Manufactured in the United States

ISBN 978.1.62619.007.8

Library of Congress CIP data applied for.

Notice: The information in this book is true and complete to the best of our knowledge. It is offered without guarantee on the part of the author or The History Press. The author and The History Press disclaim all liability in connection with the use of this book.

And I think that this music will live forever.
—*Albert French*

Contents

Contents

Foreword

Although the idea that jazz was "born in New Orleans" has become something of a cliché used to promote cultural tourism in the Crescent City, it is based in historical circumstances that are singular and compelling, to say the least. Given its French, Spanish and, especially, West African roots and its propensity for creolization, the city's culture has never conformed to the dominant contours associated with the "American experience" as routinely conceived in historical textbooks, and the emergence of jazz illustrates the difference. Yet, as Sally Newhart's rendition of the history of the Original Tuxedo Jazz Band ably illustrates, the origins of New Orleans jazz are about more than the standard mythology surrounding the antics of the pimps and hustlers in the Storyville District, although that is certainly part of the story. This book is the tale of a jazz band that has not only transcended the stereotypes but has also survived for more than a century (a feat that has never been equaled in jazz history), working its way from the black tenderloin into the homes and hearts of the city's affluent, white social elite in less than a decade. In an age of divisive racial segregation, jazz music as performed by the Original Tuxedo Jazz Band became a means of promoting mutuality and reconciliation through a shared pleasure principle based in dance, and it created relationships that subverted the dehumanizing effects of racism and lasted for generations. Such is the power of New Orleans jazz, when played from the heart.

The founder of the Original Tuxedo Band in 1910–11 was the trumpeter Oscar Celestin, whose tenure as leader lasted for almost half a century. Under his command (shared for a time with trombonist William "Bebe" Ridgley), the Tuxedo was one of the first jazz bands to record in New Orleans (in January

1925); it was instrumental in the organization of Local 496, the black American Federation of Musicians union in New Orleans (established in July 1926); it was one of the earliest jazz bands to employ women regularly (as pianists); and it built a loyal following that spanned conventional racial and ethnic categories by providing an infectious dance music that was popular among black and white audiences from the bottom of society to the top. These accomplishments were not so much the product of strategic planning as they were the result of Celestin's open-minded and endearing manner of dealing with the people he encountered in everyday life and Ridgley's reputation for dependability and business acumen. It was a formula that worked well, and it was handed down to subsequent leaders, such as the trombonist Eddie Pierson; banjoist Albert "Papa" French; his son, the drummer Bob French; and, most recently, Bob's nephew, Gerald French, also a drummer. Like so much of New Orleans culture, the history of the Tuxedo Band is about kinship and community.

In New Orleans jazz, the trick for any leader is to combine innovation with respect for tradition, juxtaposing nostalgia and surprise effectively at all times, while also serving the respective needs of dancers and listeners. Although each of the leaders of the Original Tuxedo Jazz Band brought a very personal style to bear in interpreting these imperatives, they applied the formula uniformly as required, offering a musical product that was in keeping with the city's multi-faceted festival traditions ranging from neighborhood "cutting contests," "second lines" and funerals with music, to carnival balls, debutante parties and country club dances, all united by the band's ability to show its customers a good time. This is why the Original Tuxedo Jazz Band rarely lacked bookings.

These leaders knew their audiences: in Celestin's case, it was not uncommon for him to play for three generations of the families that hired him. All the various musicians who were affiliated with the Tuxedo knew the importance of combining art with entertainment and never drew false distinctions based on ideas of purity or authenticity. They played what the people who were paying for their services wanted to hear. In fact, most New Orleans jazz band leaders subscribed to this maxim, offering business cards that read: "Music for all occasions," with "what you want, I got it!" in fine print below. Throughout its one-hundred-year history, the Original Tuxedo Jazz Band has lived up to this standard in both live performance and on its many recordings, which is why anyone interested in the history of New Orleans jazz will want to read this book.

Dr. Bruce Boyd Raeburn
Curator, Hogan Jazz Archive
Tulane University

Acknowledgements

This history was researched with the cooperation of many individuals. Dr. Bruce Boyd Raeburn, curator of the Hogan Jazz Archive; Lynn Abbott, associate curator, recorded sound; Elaina Jordan, past associate curator, graphics; and Nicole Shibata, present associate curator, graphics, helped me navigate the extensive resources of Tulane University's Hogan Jazz Archive. I am grateful for their support and encouragement.

I am indebted to Greg Lambousy, director of collections, and Elizabeth Sherwood, assistant registrar, photo requests and permissions at the Louisiana State Museum; Jarad Kim Foreman at the AFM Local 174-496; Jerry Moran, Native Orleanian Fine Photography; Freddie "Blue" Goodrich, Freddie Blue Works Photography; Gerald French, curator of the French Family Archive; and his father, George French.

I'd also like to say a heartfelt thank you to my family and friends for their patience. This is for you, Bob.

Abbreviations

a-hrn	alto horn
ap-hrn	alto peck horn
arr	arranger
as	alto saxophone
b	bass, string
bar-hrn	baritone horn
baz	bazooka
bgp	bagpipes
bj	banjo
b-d	bass drum
b-vin	bass violin
cl	clarinet
cnt	cornet
d	drum
dir	director
el-b	electric bass
el-g	electric guitar
el-p	electric piano
ent	entertainer
flh	flugelhorn
g	guitar
ldr	leader
mand	mandolin
mello	mellophonium

Abbreviations

p	piano
pic	piccolo
sax	saxophone
sop	soprano saxophone
souse	sousaphone
tb	trombone
tp	trumpet
ts	tenor saxophone
tu	tuba
vln	violin
voc	vocals

Chapter 1

Oscar "Papa" Celestin

O scar Phillip "Papa" Celestin, the first leader of the Original Tuxedo Jazz Band, was born on January 1, 1884, to an African American family living in Napoleonville, Assumption Parish, Louisiana. The youngest of thirteen children, he lived with his parents in the small, rural town located fifty-six miles west of New Orleans. His father, a transient sugar cane cutter, supported the family by working as a field hand on plantations in the Napoleonville area, which had a population of seventy-three by the 1890 census. The Celestins were one of many poor black and Creole families in the area, and when young Oscar was old enough, he went to work with his father in the sugar cane fields, as had all the other children in his family.

Interested in music from an early age, Oscar had been attempting to teach himself to play the more readily available guitar and mandolin, but all that changed when he accompanied his father onto a Mississippi riverboat and heard a riverboat band. From the moment he heard the sound of those horns, all he wanted was to play the cornet. He started saving every penny with the dream of buying one but was spared the long wait when a co-worker on the plantation passed along an old battered cornet after hearing that young Celestin wanted one.

His parents arranged for him to take music lessons from Professor Claiborne Williams, a music teacher that lived about ten miles away in Donaldsonville, Ascension Parish. Williams, the cornetist for the St. Joseph Brass Band, which he had organized and led, was a classically trained violinist but taught all instruments, charging fifty cents for a lesson that could last up to an hour. John G. Curran, a music promoter, told

David Hillyer, "I guess the first jazz band in the world was the Claiborne Williams band from Donaldsonville, Louisiana." He traveled by boat on Bayou Lafourche to get to his students, who would gather in groups at the different plantations along the bayou for their weekly lesson. In a short amount of time, young Celestin started playing with local bands at neighborhood parties and church picnics.

While he wanted nothing more than to be a musician, his mother encouraged him to get, and keep, a day job so he would have a reliable means of supporting himself. He found a job as a cook on the Texas-Pacific Railroad and left Napoleonville to move to St. Charles Parish. By 1902, he was playing in his first band, the J.C. Trist Band, named for the man who bought the instruments. While he was in St. Charles Parish, he adopted the nickname of "Sonny" and was soon playing cornet with another local St. Charles Parish boys' marching brass band, the Indiana Brass Band, led by cornetist Walter Kenchen.

In 1906, twenty-two-year-old Celestin moved to New Orleans, where the population of three hundred thousand included twenty percent black, a far cry from the mostly black population of less than one thousand in Napoleonville. His first order of business was to get a job. At six foot four and weighing close to three hundred pounds, he had no trouble getting hired as a longshoreman and was soon working on the docks. In his later years, he was happy to talk about his longshoreman's union card and the good times he spent on and near the Mississippi River.

With his day job secured, Celestin concentrated on getting to know the city and getting to be known as a musician. New Orleans was full of young musicians, and there were lots of opportunities for a talented cornet player. He played spot jobs with a number of other up-and-coming musicians in the city: Jack Carey, Joe Oliver, Jimmie Noone, Bunk Johnson, Peter Bocage, Jimmy Palao and Jelly Roll Morton. He played cornet with the Imperial Band, was a regular in the Crescent Orchestra and would occasionally take a job with the Olympia Orchestra, formed by Freddie Keppard in 1907.

By 1908, more than a year after the legendary cornetist Buddy Bolden had played his last known job with Henry "Red" Allen's Brass Band, a marching band based in Algiers, Louisiana, Celestin was playing cornet with them. The band was always in demand for picnics, funerals and other church or social events.

Then in 1909, Celestin took the final step to becoming a full-time musician when he was hired by Alderman Tom Anderson, a political leader in the fourth ward, to work in his saloon at 209 Basin Street. Anderson's Fair Play Saloon was one of many on Basin Street, the gateway to Storyville.

The Storyville District in New Orleans, commonly called "the District," was within the area bordered by Iberville Street, St. Louis Street, Basin Street and Claiborne Avenue. The wood-framed buildings that lined the streets provided all forms of evening entertainment, but the primary focus was on the business of prostitution, which, while technically illegal, had been tolerated since 1897 and would continue to be until November 1917. Most of the more elegant "sporting houses" had beautifully furnished reception areas where the male customers were able to meet the women that worked the evenings. Pianos were the instrument of choice to provide background music, and talented piano players were well paid and always in demand.

Over at the Globe Hall, just outside the District in the Treme at St. Claude and St. Peter Streets, near the present location of the New Orleans Municipal Auditorium, Manuel "Fess" Manetta was getting $2.50 for playing the piano from 8:00 p.m. until 4:00 a.m., with an extra $1.00 for playing the advertising from 1:00 p.m. to 6:00 p.m. before the evening's dance.

Drinking, gambling and dancing were the other forms of entertainment offered in the District, where the poorly paved streets were lined with bars and dance halls. The one- and two-story buildings always had bars and usually bandstands, where musicians were able to enjoy steady employment. As the only jukeboxes were nickel cylinder players in drug stores, and never in saloons, if there was going to be music, it was going to be live, and just as it continues in modern New Orleans, if there's music, there will be dancing—no matter the size of the place.

The Slow Drag was a popular dance when the music was slow and bluesy. Couples would press their bodies tightly together and keep time with the music in a smooth bump and grind. The couple could move forward, backward or side to side, always starting on the first and third beat of the measure. If you stepped forward with the right foot, you dragged the left foot. If you stepped to the left you would drag the right foot. Bands would accommodate the dancers with "Sunflower Slow Drag" and "Make Me a Pallet on the Floor," though most any song could be played at that slow tempo. Drummer Josiah "Cie" Frazier reflected, "You could hear the heels of the people just smoothing down on the ground like that."

"High Society," "Bucket's Got a Hole in It," "Down Home Rag" and "Liza Jane" were some of the other frequently requested tunes that every musician knew. The bands played from eight in the evening until four in the morning. They were compensated with free wine and between $1.50

and $2.50 per musician, with the band's manager getting $3.00. The real money was in tips, and a hot band in a popular club could easily collect $15.00 per person in an evening. This was during a time when a loaf of bread cost five cents.

The Tuxedo Dance Hall, owned by brothers Charlie and Harry Parker, was one of the more popular dance halls. According to the *Daily Picayune* of March 25, 1913:

> *The Tuxedo, a model of the dance halls which make up a good part of the Tenderloin, occupies a berth on North Franklin, between Bienville and Iberville. The bar faces the street and opens, without screens, the full width of the part apportioned to it onto the street. At the lower end of the hall a stand has been erected for the music, about 12 feet above the dancing floor, and is connected with it by a small, narrow stairway. Here a negro band holds forth and from about 8 o'clock at night until 4 o'clock in the morning plays varied rags, conspicuous for being the latest in popular music, interspersed with compositions by the musicians themselves. The band has a leader who grotesquely prompts the various pieces, which generally constitute several brass pieces, a violin, guitar, piccolo, and a piano.*

When the Tuxedo had changed from a brothel to a dance hall, the Parker brothers hired Manuel "Fess" Manetta, a well-respected piano player, to assemble the best band in the city. His choice of musicians included: Peter Bocage (vln), George Fihle (tb), Arnold Metoyer (tp), Luis "Papa" Tio (cl), Babb Frank (pic) and Nooky Johnson (ent). They strictly read from sheet music and didn't play by ear or improvise.

When Metoyer's health failed, the band went three weeks without a regular cornet player because they had to have a musician that could read music. They couldn't hire a non-reader, even if that non-reader was a good player like Manuel Perez.

Manetta recommended Oscar Celestin, who lived uptown, worked on the railroad, was a reader and had played with Jack Carey, the man who had developed the "Tiger Rag." George Fihle remembered working with Celestin in a parade and agreed with Manetta that he would be a good choice. So when Manetta and Babb Frank, thought to be the best piccolo player in the city, got off work at 3:00 p.m., they briefly went by the Big 25, another club located about a block up Franklin Street, and then on to Celestin's home to try and hire him. Celestin was agreeable and went to work at the Tuxedo Dance Hall the next night.

Manetta did his best to make Celestin's first night playing with the band easier. The band opened with "Kinklets," a Scott Joplin tune that Celestin had played with Jack Carey's band. The next song was "The Flowers that Bloom in the Spring," another tune Celestin knew. When the band quit for the night, Celestin took their written orchestrations home and practiced during the day.

In 1910, when Celestin was hired, the Tuxedo Dance Hall's house band consisted of Celestin (cnt), George Filhe (tb), Peter Bocage (vln), Lorenzo Tio Jr. (cl), T. Brouchard (b), Manuel Manetta (p) and Louis Cottrell (d). Celestin, a compelling vocalist and good all-around performer, was soon made leader of the band. Taking his inspiration from the name of the club, he started calling the band the Tuxedo Orchestra.

He was becoming a well-known personality, as reported in the New Orleans *Daily Picayune*: "The leader of the band at The Tuxedo was the pride of the house. Harry Lauder, Billy Van or George Evans never had anything on him in funny facial expressions or funny twists of the legs. When he led the band people stopped to watch his antics…"

Competition between the various clubs was a given, and anything a band or bandleader could do to encourage more customers to walk through the door would not only add money to the tip jar, but it would also keep the club owner happy, thereby ensuring the band steady employment. Some other dance halls operating in the District between 1910 and 1913 and vying for a packed house each night were Fewclothes Cabaret on Basin Street, which featured Tig Chambers when he wasn't playing at the Big 25 on Franklin Street; the Globe Hall, where the Eagle Band played; Hanan's Cabaret on Liberty Street, which had Freddy Keppard and his Olympia Orchestra; and Manuel Perez at Rice's Café on Marais Street. You would find King Oliver at Huntz Cabaret on Liberty Street, Pete Lala's on Marais Street had the Bunk Johnson Band and over at the 101 Ranch Dance Hall on Franklin Street, which was owned by Billy Phillips, you could listen to the Silver Leaf Orchestra, with William "Bebe" Ridgley on trombone.

Chapter 2

William "Bebe" Ridgley

William "Bebe" Ridgley was born on January 15, 1882, on Sundorn Road, in Metairie, Louisiana, near the present-day causeway in Jefferson Parish. Metairie, a suburb of New Orleans that is now congested with homes and vehicles, was nothing more than vast acres of farmland spotted with dairy farms and the occasional small cluster of wood-framed homes. The United States Census for 1900 lists Jefferson Parish having a total population of 15,321, while the bordering Orleans Parish had a population of 287,104.

There were thirteen children in the family, with William being the oldest of the two boys and two girls still living at home when his mother died while giving birth to twins. Both babies also died within days of being born. At the close of his first year in school, William had been promoted to the second grade, but with the sudden change to his family's situation, he felt that he should not return to school when classes started in the fall. He chose instead to go to work to help support the family. So at the age of ten, Ridgley found a job with a German family who owned a small grocery store a short walk from his home in what was still considered "the country" in Jefferson Parish.

The store's owner hired a lot of young workers, and the combination of a bunch of kids hanging around a quiet country store with little to do and a German family with a love of music living in an area where a musical career was well respected led to the inevitable—"Let's start a band!" Encouraged by the grocer, the young group of employees soon put together a band with a banjo, a clarinet, a cornet, drums and Ridgley's bass violin. The grocer, who believed in the importance of music lessons, hired James B. Humphrey, an established New Orleans trumpet player and music instructor, to teach his employees. Humphrey taught music to children in the city of New Orleans from his home at the corner of Valance and Liberty Streets. He also traveled by train to teach a weekly music lesson to the children of field hands on the Magnolia, Deer Range, Bell Aire and Ironton plantations.

He agreed to travel the short distance over the line into Jefferson Parish to teach the grocer's group. Every Sunday morning, Ridgley would take the grocer's two-wheeled spring cart to Liberty Street in New Orleans to pick up their music teacher, making it back to the grocery store for the band's 9:00 a.m. music lesson.

"Professor Jim" was known for his ability to teach a band fast and would bring a new piece of music each week with every instrument's part written out. He started them off with simple arrangements of familiar tunes, hymns they had grown up with and popular songs. As the band members progressed, their interests were more in marches rather than dance music. The dozen or so young fellows admired marching brass bands and wanted to form one.

Humphrey suggested to Ridgley that while he was a competent bass violin player, he might be better off learning the trombone, especially if his plan was to be in a marching brass band. So one night a week for about a year and a half, Ridgley made the trip to the Professor's Liberty Street home for a private lesson. In an interview with William Russell in 1959, Ridgley remembered the first tune he learned on the trombone was "Harmony Rag."

The German family that owned the store where he worked found a C.G. Conn one-valve trombone, which they purchased for $85.00 and gave to Ridgley as a gift. He progressed with the instrument and was soon glad he had made the switch as the band of youngsters started to get small jobs in the area.

The band at the store would practice most nights, which kept the place crowded all the time. Other local bands would make it a point to pass by the store on their way to their parades, funerals and house or club gigs. Bands coming from a distance on the way to New Orleans for a gig knew they'd get a friendly welcome at the store. Ridgley, whom the German family treated like one of their own, had the privilege of being able to take in the musicians he knew and give them a cool drink of water or some whiskey. The sound of a band travels pretty well in the relatively quiet countryside, and there would soon be a crowd listening to a few songs before the band continued on its way. It was a great situation all the way around. The store made extra sales, the bands played some advertising with hopes of future gigs, the locals had a place to hear music and the grocery store band was able to learn the music that was fresh and popular in their impromptu lessons from those traveling musicians.

Sometime around the turn of the century, Ridgley and his family moved across the parish line into Orleans Parish and made a home on General Ogden Street in the Carrollton area. The grocery store band started getting hired to play for some of the smaller white parties in the Carrollton area, and at one of those dances, Ridgley hired Buddy Bolden to play cornet. Bolden was living with some of his kin on Hillary Street in the Carrollton area. Ridgley didn't think Bolden could read music very well, but he thought he was a wonderful fellow with a style of his own.

It was and still is a common practice for musicians to have a nickname, not necessarily one they would choose for themselves but more frequently one chosen by their colleagues. Nicknames were most often inspired by a physical attribute, but they could be based on anything. One of Ridgley's sisters had always called him her baby. During the time they were playing in the Carrollton area Ridgley, with a little help from his band members, started going by "Bebe," pronounced "Baybay."

With years of practice and playing together, the band had become a cohesive unit with its own signature sound. Whenever it hired a substitute musician to fill in on a gig, that musician would be required to play in the style of the band to maintain the band's identity. That constant sharing of musical styles made it possible to find musicians that could play in the style of any band. When the leader and cornet player in Ridgley's band died, there was a short period of inactivity before Henry Lambert, an older tuba player who also played the valve trombone, reorganized the band and, as their leader and manager, kept them active with bookings for a while.

When the band dissolved for the final time, their most recent cornet player, Professor Frank Welsh (or Welch), convinced the rest of the players to go to New Orleans where he had found a job at the 101 Ranch playing with the Silver Leaf Orchestra led by Albert Baptiste, a classically trained violinist. Welsh was sure he would be able to help some of his old band members secure jobs with the Silver Leaf or one of the many other local New Orleans bands.

In 1910, Ridgley left his family, moved to the city of New Orleans and was soon hired to play bass violin with the Silver Leaf Orchestra, a "reading" band that played waltzes and popular songs from sheet music. When Ridgley became a member of the band some of the older forms of dance music, like the quadrille or the mazurka, were still played. Most of the evening music included waltzes, which had been introduced to New Orleans in 1802, or ragtime, with dances like the One-Step, the Grizzly Bear, the Turkey Trot and the Bunny Hop. Often a quadrille would be played as the last dance before the midnight buffet, after which the older patrons were ready to call it a night and leave. The Slow Drag remained the most popular dance after the old folks left.

At the 101 Ranch one night, Adam Lambert, the band's trombone player, suggested that he and Ridgley, who had been hired to play the bass, trade instruments. With that simple act, Ridgley made the permanent switch to playing trombone. As a trombone player, he used the brass instrument to play the familiar string bass line, take the lead or, most often, harmonize with other horns and fill in open spots.

Ridgley had learned from "Professor Jim" Humphrey to play the Bb/F one-valve trombone, sometimes called a trill-valve trombone. This was a non-slide trombone and was the same style trombone Lambert played. Though Baptiste DeLisle, a valve trombone master, had been playing the more modern Bb slide trombone since his return from Cuba in 1899, Ridgley said the first slide trombone player he saw was George Fihle, who played with Celestin in the District. Later he saw a slide trombone being played by a musician named Sergeant Tucker. Manuel Manetta said his Uncle Norman "Deuce" Manetta was the first slide trombone player seen in New Orleans.

Professor Welsh, the band's cornet player, thought all that sliding made for a much more exciting performance that the club patrons would love. It didn't take much for him to convince Ridgley to buy himself a new sliding trombone and add some extra showmanship to his performance.

At that time, most clubs paid the same wages, and bands would be associated with a specific club. The Silver Leaf Orchestra playing at the 101 Ranch had the same pay scale as the Tuxedo Orchestra a block away at the Tuxedo Dance Hall. Each musician was paid $1.50 to play from 8:00 p.m. until 4:00 a.m., plus as much as they could make in tips. The managers of the bands were always looking for the chance to hire out for private functions at homes, restaurants and private clubs. When the band played a private dance, it played for three hours, and the pay was $2.50 a man, with the manager getting $3.00.

There was yet another common New Orleans practice that gave the band a way to add to their income: the advertising job. When a band was hired for an advertising job, the music and venue were quite different than the usual dance or club date. In most cases, an advertising job required the band to hire a mule-drawn flatbed or a furniture wagon and then ride around town with placards or banners festooning the wagon announcing the business

An early 1920s band ready to roll on an advertising job. *Courtesy of the Hogan Jazz Archive, Tulane University.*

to which they were drawing attention. While the mule pulled the wagon around, the band members would distribute handbills. When the wagon was stationary, the band would perform. The music played wasn't the more predictable dance music of the nightclubs. Rather, it was more emotional, with new improvisations to the tunes being created spontaneously as the musicians played "by ear" in a "gut-bucket" style, similar to barrelhouse, with a strong beat and a rollicking delivery. The band's job was to attract attention, and this music was invented to gather a crowd.

Ridgley was introduced to Celestin when the Silver Leaf's cornet player, Professor Frank Welsh, wanted to quit the band. Welsh suggested Ridgley ask Celestin to take his place, saying he was a likable, talented player, and he arranged for the men to meet. It was decided that Celestin would sit in with the Silver Leaf Orchestra, which at that time consisted of Celestin (cnt), Ridgley (tb), Lorenzo Tio Jr. (cl), Jean Vigne Jr. (p) and Louis Cottrell Sr. (d). There was no bass, banjo or guitar. Ridgley said that while Celestin occasionally played with him at the 101 Ranch, he never played with Celestin at the Tuxedo Dance Hall, where Celestin continued to lead the Tuxedo Orchestra.

Ridgley remarked that while both the Silver Leaf and the Tuxedo Orchestra were reading bands, the Silver Leaf sounded different than the Tuxedo because the men in the Silver Leaf would also practice with a gramophone and mimic the style of whatever they heard. They could play the blues and dance music, whatever was popular and recorded. In contrast, the men in the Tuxedo were readers who solely used sheet music available at the music stores in New Orleans or, if necessary, could be special ordered from New York.

Chapter 3
New Orleans Music Culture

New Orleans music is based on the traditional music of the ethnic groups that shared their cultures with the city. It was a place where all ethnic and racial groups were represented and enjoyed the ability to interact and a place where the different rhythms and playing styles were shared by all the musicians as they gradually merged into the distinct American regional music with its African American core that we know as jazz.

The early occupations of the Spanish and French, before 1803 when the Louisiana Purchase was accomplished by the United States, brought the quadrille, a form of French ballroom dancing similar to American square dancing, where four couples interact in a square-shaped formation. The Italian, German and Irish immigrants contributed polkas, schottisches and the mazurka, a lively partnered dance with Polish origins similar to a polka and played in three-quarter time.

Long considered the most northern port of the Caribbean, New Orleans, actually in the Gulf of Mexico, acquired a bit of Caribbean culture with each shipment of rum, coffee and bananas. As early as the 1700s, the Spanish, French and native inhabitants of the islands in the Caribbean had been immigrating through the Port of New Orleans, with many staying in the city.

Louisiana was a slave-owning state where plantations that grew sugar cane, cotton and other products lined the banks of the Mississippi River and outlying bayous. The thousands of African men, women and children imported against their will and sold at auction in the city of New Orleans struggled to hold on to the comfort of their traditions in the hell of their daily lives as slaves. The laws of Louisiana permitted Sunday gatherings where slaves were allowed to trade with each other, sing their spiritual music and dance to their traditional tribal rhythms. In New Orleans, this weekly gathering was held in Congo Square, now known as Armstrong Park. Permission to engage with one another added a dimension to the local music that was not to be found in other slave-owning states, where the slaves' native cultures were not respected.

In May 1796, during the last decade of the Spanish Colonial era, the first opera was staged in New Orleans at the Theatre St. Pierre on St. Peter Street, between Royal and Bourbon Streets. French, Italian and German operas often premiered in New Orleans in the many opera theaters located in both the French and American parts of the city, where they enjoyed the constant support of the residents of the city. The French Opera House, on Bourbon Street at Toulouse Street, opened in 1859 and was extremely popular until it burned to the ground on December 4, 1919. When David Hillyer interviewed Charles L. Dufour he said, "Everybody in New Orleans. That was one thing they did. They went to the Opera House. They lived in the Opera House virtually." In the late 1800s, operas, dances, street parades, picnics and church functions continued to be the most common forms of social interaction. The one ingredient they all included was music. Dance bands were commonly led by violinists and consisted of highly skilled French or Creole musicians classically trained to read music. They played to polite society audiences who sat and listened or danced to the popular waltzes, polkas and quadrilles.

The Creole musicians, born on American soil with their mix of African and European heritage, lived downtown on the downriver side of Canal Street. While there were significant numbers of Spanish, German, Italian and Irish immigrants, the most prevalent mix of cultures was the combination of French and black with its own dialect of Creole French. Classical musical training was considered very important in the French-based culture and was started at an early age.

The Americans, who had taken ownership of the area in 1803 after the Louisiana Purchase, settled in the sector of the city on the upriver side of Canal Street, and while they enjoyed music, they were not as driven as the Europeans to train their children in a classical manner.

Black musicians in the city were either free people of color who had migrated to the city or they were recently freed slaves who had minimal education of any sort, let alone a classical music education. Most did not or could barely read music but improvised using their own traditional rhythms and syncopations.

In the aftermath of the War Between the States and the end of slavery, society and politicians struggled to create rules and structure in the city. The Louisiana Legislature passed Code 111 in 1894, which declared that Creoles had the same status as blacks and removed the rights and privileges they had enjoyed as free people of color. Neither blacks nor Creoles were accepted in white society as equals, and each were expected to keep to their own racial group.

Classically trained, downtown Creole musicians were thrown together with improvising uptown black musicians. Abby Foster, a drummer, felt there was animosity between the uptown and the downtown musicians, though Albert Nicholas, a reed player, disagreed and indicated they worked together well. Some problems arose from the competition for jobs, but generally, if an orchestra or band used printed sheet music, it would only be interested in hiring readers. As the twentieth century began, black children were being sent by their parents to the same music teachers as the Creole children in hopes of providing them with equal opportunities.

Unlike Ridgley, who was a member of the new generation of black musicians who had obtained a structured music education, most of the old-time trombone players didn't read music. Instead, they would make up or fake their parts, relying on their ears to tell them what to play. If a musician could figure out a melody from a written orchestration, he would make up the other parts. Many musicians, such as clarinetist Zeb Lenois, would learn the melodies from recorded music and help the other musicians in the band make up their own parts. In an interview with Richard Allen, Ridgley said, "It would take a band about two to five hours to learn a tune, and after they learned it they always played it the same way. There were no brass bands that played entirely by head, not even uptown. Somebody had to be able to read. They always played some fake numbers though."

Thomas "Mutt" Carey, a cornet player who had originally started as a drummer, was known to make up tunes while on the bandstand working a job. He would teach the band as they were playing, and before the job was over, the band would be playing the tune. "They'd make up songs and play them and sometimes an hour later if you asked them to play it again, they couldn't do it," recounted "Black Happy" Goldston.

As non-reading musicians were passed over by bandleaders, they realized they needed lessons to become readers and therefore qualify for more job opportunities. Louis Cottrell Jr., who played clarinet and saxophone with Ridgley's Tuxedo Jazz Band in the late 1920s, explained how important it is to have the classical training, but how jazz is so much more than that.

When a guy started off, he would start off always training in the classics. It was the rudiments of music you go through the school, you understand. You would really get the basic foundation. Well, generally, if you have the training, just like if you have your alphabet, you learn how to read you can play any type of music. But, it's a difference in the jazz field because that's you, you improvising on the thoughts and memories and thoughts of your own. Not copied from somebody else. But, again, it is comparable because you take everything. This guy that's ever played a horn and is considered a jazz musician. He's playing something someone already has done. It's just that he improve or improvise on it…and then he has a little something that he puts in that may be a little different, but it's something someone already has done. It's just like, if you, say if you an orator, see, the time comes when you have a speech or something, you just putting down notes and you elaborate on those notes and as he's going he's building up and I mean it's just part of him. Not that he planned it. It's the same way with a jazz musician. Depends on his audience, depends on the mood he's in, and that's the way it is. Individual. Depends on the individual. And of course you have good and better and best in everything. It's a real good one and a better one and you have one that you just can't beat.

The youngsters they always have time for something new. A musician, when he's coming up, is always thinking of something new so he can out do his competitors. Or to stay ahead of his competition. But after you reach a certain age, you're not going through those studies or putting in the time, because you have other obligation[s]. That come about especially when you're a grandfather. You know, it's not like the fellow who's just starting out. All he can visualize is more. When I reach that peak. Or when I can do this, or if I can get through this touchy part. What am I going to do? Well, I better do this and do that. Because you've got to think of that. You're thinking just of the dollar and of course, you want to give service to get that dollar. One thing I must say is the training that I received from home, the training that I received from [Lorenzo] *Tio, is this: Never worry about the money. If you can produce, money will follow.*

Peter Bocage, who played the cornet, trombone, violin and banjo with many different bands including Buddy Bolden's, agreed there was a difference between a trained and a non-trained musician. In an interview with Barry Martin he explained:

It's a different feeling and everything there, you see. And cause the man that's polished is bound to be different from the man that's in the rough, understand? Why, sho' absolutely—that's all that is. And that's all the difference in gut-bucket. It's just getting a gut-bucket man and a gut-bucket tune, and you got gut-bucket, you see. But the other man would play the same thing, but it wouldn't be exactly, because they, it's two different men there, see? There's two different thoughts, two different feelings, you understand? One guy can't play bad if he wanted, 'cause he learnt right, see? The other guy can't play right because he can't, he don't know what he's doing. He's just blowing, that's all, see? That's the whole thing in a nutshell, right there, you see?

By 1900, the music scene was already changing to include more brass band marches, ragtime and blues. Musicians were playing to a younger set of dancers who craved the more expressive and spontaneous style that included less sight-reading and encouraged more improvisational playing. The first New Orleans jazz bands were combining and hybridizing the instrumentations of the string band and the brass marching band. The six-piece band that this created had a front line of cornet, trombone and clarinet playing with the rhythm section of guitar or banjo, bass and drums. The music these bands were playing was looser, with a combination of musicians that could read and those who improvised. Louis Cottrell Jr. said, "There would be pianos in the clubs and on the advertising trucks, [but] not when they marched 'cause they couldn't carry them."

Chapter 4

Murder at the Tuxedo Dance Hall

On Easter Monday, March 24, 1913, at about 4:30 a.m., Billy Phillips, the owner of the 101 Ranch Dance Hall, went to the Tuxedo Dance Hall to meet with Harry Parker, one of the owners, to try to resolve a quarrel they had been having. The men were sitting at the bar when Charles Harrison, a New York hoodlum on the lam working as a waiter at the Tuxedo, stepped behind Phillips and fired at his back. In the gunfight that followed, Phillips, Parker and three other men were killed.

The *Times-Picayune* reported that there were officially no musicians playing at the Tuxedo that Sunday night. While the bars never closed to their drinking patrons, there was a local custom of no music from midnight Saturday until the band started playing at 8:00 p.m. Monday night.

Manetta and Bocage agree there had been a small pick-up band, without any brass, playing that night consisting of Manetta (p), Bocage (vln), Luis "Papa" Tio (cl) and Louis Cottrell Sr. (d). They escaped out the back door.

The *Times-Picayune* reported that public outrage in the days after the murders led New Orleans superintendent James W. Reynolds to call for the prompt closing of all dance halls in the city and the revoking of all permits. Commissioner Newman sided with the majority of the public and heartily approved Reynolds's wish to clear the city of all such places.

With the Tuxedo Dance Hall closed because of the murders, Celestin joined Ridgley at the 101 Ranch Dance Hall, which continued to operate for a short time before the city shut down the entire district. Ridgley recalls the members of that band being Celestin (cnt), Ridgley (tb), Lorenzo Tio Jr. (cl), Jean Vigne (p) and Louis Cottrell Sr. (d).

With the dance halls closed, the musicians who had enjoyed steady employment found themselves vying for jobs scattered in the city. Celestin waited to see if the dance halls would open again, thereby resolving the problem, but it soon became apparent they would not. He pulled together a band that he led on cornet with Eddie Atkins (tb), Louis "Big Eye" Nelson (cl), Joe Howard (cnt), Manuel Manetta (p) and Warren "Baby" Dodds (d). They started playing a regular gig at the Villa Café. Ridgley went with Amos Riley, a trumpet player, and jobbed around the city.

In 1914, some of the dance halls and sporting houses reopened. Ridgley, with his trombone, and Celestin, with his cornet, had gotten together again with Johnny Lindsay (tb, b), Lorenzo Tio Jr.(cl), Adolph "Tats" Alexander Jr.(cl, sax, bar-hrn), Peter Bocage (vln), Tom Benton (g, bj, mand, p), Ernest Trepagnier (d) and Clarence Williams, who sang, played piano and helped with bookings. They called themselves the Tuxedo Jazz Band and were able to find steady work at the newly reopened 101 Ranch.

Armand Piron, a violinist, and Clarence Williams, a piano player, jointly owned the Piron-Williams Music Publishing Company on Tulane Avenue, which by 1916 had begun to lose business to more popular publishing houses in Chicago and New York City. To attract some attention, they joined with Celestin's band, hoping to become one of the first black bands to play the Orpheum Vaudeville Circuit. Martin Beck's Orpheum Vaudeville Circuit, one of the largest, had contracts with forty-five vaudeville theaters in thirty-six cities in the United States and Canada and was always looking for new musical and theatrical acts.

The band included Celestin (tp), Ridgely (tb), Jimmie Noone (cl), Armand Piron (vln), Johnny St. Cyr (bj), John Lindsay (b), Clarence Williams (p), Ernest Trepagnier (d) and Tom Benton (bj, g, voc). The members rehearsed and took publicity shots, but the contract never materialized and Williams left for Chicago and later New York to promote the publishing company.

As Ridgely remembers, "In the publicity picture of the vaudeville group, Piron was there though not a member of the band that was to perform. Tom Benton is pictured holding the smaller mandolin/banjo. He played the guitar, banjo and mandolin and all very well. He was a good singer and good ragtime player, which meant he could play and improvise by ear. Johnny St. Cyr is holding the larger banjo."

At the height of World War I, with hundreds of troops stationed in the port of New Orleans just a streetcar ride away from the Storyville District, the U.S. Department of the Navy, struggling with an epidemic

Piron-Williams Band, circa 1916. *Standing, left to right:* Jimmy Noone, William Ridgley, Oscar Celestin and John Lindsay. *Seated, left to right:* Ernest Trepagnier, Armand Piron, Tom Benton and Johnny St. Cyr. *Front:* Clarence Williams. *Courtesy of the Hogan Jazz Archive, Tulane University.*

of venereal disease, threatened to close the district with or without the city's cooperation. On October 2, 1917, with pressure from the navy and the general population of the city, New Orleans mayor Martin Behrman, against the wishes of the city government, closed the district for the final time. The loss of steady dance hall work meant the bands had to go "out into the field" and scramble for gigs.

Celestin and Ridgley gathered a band consisting of John Lindsay (tb), Lorenzo Tio Jr. (cl), Peter Bocage (vln) and Ernest Trepagnier (d). They continued to use the Tuxedo Jazz Band as their name, and Celestin became the leader and musical director, the one who runs the band while it's on the stand. Ridgley had the position of being the band's business manager and booking agent, the one who interacted with the public, found and booked the jobs and collected the money. Ridgley owned a pressing shop and shoe black stand on Howard Avenue between Dryades and Baronne Streets, which soon became the headquarters for the band.

He said that when he took over as manager of the Tuxedo Band it wasn't strange for him as he'd been working with white people all his life. Ridgley said, "I was well trained with that good old 'Dixie' training, knew my place, and tried to be a nice colored fellow."

Ridgley was booking jobs around the city and in outlying areas when an opportunity for steady employment arose with his friend Jack Sheehan, a man who knew his way around the horse-racing and gambling worlds.

Sheehan, whose real name was Mark Boasberg, had purchased the abandoned Whitehall Plantation just out of town on the River Road. Built in 1857, it had been owned and occupied by Francois Pascalis de LaBarre IV until the Civil War and then left abandoned until the family lost it in the 1892 sheriff's sale, when Sheehan bought it. He converted it into a nightclub he named the Suburban Gardens. An easy drive from New Orleans, it became popular with the drinking, gambling and jazz-loving crowd that thrived in an extravagant party atmosphere. It was known as the "roadhouse in the country" and was the site of the Tuxedo Jazz Band's next steady job.

The band Celestin and Ridgley put together consisted of Celestin (cnt), Ridgley (tb), Lorenzo Tio (cl), Peter Bocage (vln), Johnny St. Cyr (bj) and Louis Cottrell Sr. (d).

In late 1917 or early 1918, Ridgley and Celestin reorganized the band and changed the name to the Tuxedo Orchestra. The band consisted of Celestin (cnt), Ridgely (tb), Sam Dutrey Sr. (cl), Paul "Polo" Barnes (sax), John Marrero or Tom Benton (bj), George "Pops" Foster or Simon Marrero (b), Emma Barrett (p) and Henry Zeno (d). Whenever Barnes was out of town, Bill Willigan, another saxophone player, took his place in the line.

Chapter 5

Tuxedos for the Tuxedo Jazz Band

One of the individual jobs the band booked was with Mr. Sim Black, an uptown swell and scoutmaster with Boy Scout Troop 13. He hired the band to play a dance during a Boy Scout weekend event in Kentwood, Louisiana. The band spent the day with the Boy Scouts playing music, eating and having an all-around good time. That evening, they were hired by a Mr. Fields at the People's Drug Store in Kentwood to play a private party for his customers. The band was so well received that it was able to book house parties at most of the Scouts' homes over the next few months.

Sim Black was impressed with the band and wanted to see them become more successful. He suggested they change the band's name to the Original Tuxedo Jazz Band and encouraged them to start wearing actual tuxedos, with white shirts, black ties and black derby hats to capitalize on the tuxedo theme. Henry Zeno, the band's drummer, found a tailor shop on Rampart Street where the owner was willing to sell them used tuxedos for fifteen dollars a piece. The band negotiated a deal wherein the tailor agreed to outfit the men in the suits in exchange for having the band play an advertising job for his shop.

In most cases, an advertising job required the band to hire a flatbed wagon, but this advertising job was different. To pay off their refurbished tuxedos, the Original Tuxedo Jazz Band assembled on the balcony above the shop and played to the people passing below for an agreed-upon amount of time over a series of weeks.

After the band members earned the tuxedos, they wore them for every job, even in the stifling 100-degree heat and 100 percent humidity of the New Orleans summers. The band's distinctive attire, its name and its instrumental style, which focused more on the mood of the music and less on the need to see how loud, fast or high a note could be played, helped them secure more society bookings. Their music was well suited to polite occasions that called for dancing and listening.

Ridgley, as manager, made it a habit to check the society pages of the *New Orleans Times-Picayune* and the *State's Item* to find out which families were planning debutante parties and balls, who was newly engaged and which Mardi Gras krewes or Social Aid and Pleasure Clubs needed a band for their events during carnival season. He worked the phone from his office at the shoe black stand and kept the band busy.

The band had a steady stream of bookings for every type of church or private function that required music and worked locally and throughout the Gulf states. While the band members never had any racially charged trouble, even in "cracker towns," being a black band during segregation meant they weren't able to stay in any of the hotels where they played. Sleeping in railroad stations where the mosquitoes would eat them up was sometimes their only option.

Chapter 6
Louis Armstrong

As early as 1915, Celestin had "ulcers of the stomach," according to Ridgley, and was often sick and not able to play. He would leave the Tuxedo for an occasional spot job or short-term job that might involve travel with another band. Celestin and George Jones, a bass player, put a band together and booked jobs that occasionally interfered with Celestin's obligations to the Tuxedo, and he would end up missing the Tuxedo jobs.

Ridgley, who respected Celestin's position as co-leader, would pay Celestin off and then hire another trumpet player for the band. Whenever he got ready to come back, Ridgley would make an opening for him. It was an understanding the two men had because they had started together and were both country boys.

During the times when Celestin was unavailable, Ridgley would fill his spot with any number of cornet players. One was Amos White, who later played with the Tuxedo Brass Band. Another was Amos Riley, who led his own band, the Tulane Orchestra, but would fill in, especially after World War I. Arnold Metoyer also filled in for Celestin and was a good cornet player, but Ridgley admitted the Tuxedo didn't care too much about him. Another was Buddy Petit, who William Ridgley said "drank and was hard to get along with. When he was sober he was all right, but if he felt like drinking he didn't care what kind of a job you have, he'd just go to sleep and wouldn't send nobody."

Ridgley found himself in need of a cornet player in 1914 or 1915 when one of the local social clubs hired the Tuxedo Band for its annual trip to the Milneburg resort area on the edge of Lake Pontchartrain. The club needed

Tuxedo Jazz Band on the Canal Street Dock, 1923. *Seated, left to right*: Henry Julian, Sam Hall, Willard Thoumy, Lawrence Marrero and John Marrero. *Standing, left to right:* Abby Foster, Milford Dolliole and William Ridgley. *Courtesy of the New Orleans Jazz Club Collection of the Louisiana State Museum.*

a brass band—basically the orchestra band without a piano—to play on the train ride out to Lake Pontchartrain. They wanted the entire orchestra to play for the Saturday night dance, Sunday at various times during the day and the Sunday night dance.

They band members were to meet the members at their club in the 300 block of North Dupre on Saturday morning and march the three blocks to Canal Street, where they would board the train to take them to Spanish Fort. The Spanish Fort had been built by Baron Carondelet in 1770 as an actual fort to defend Bayou St. John. By 1920, it was a tourist destination with easy access by the streetcar lines that covered the city. It offered beach access to Lake Pontchartrain, a hotel, a theater and a casino.

The most important instruments for the march to the train were the drums and cornet. And Celestin wasn't available.

Ridgley asked Joe Oliver if he could make the gig, but Oliver was busy. However, he said he had a "good scholar he would send," a boy who was living at the Colored Waifs Home at 5420 Franklin Avenue, whom Oliver said was a capable musician.

On Saturday morning, the rest of the band was waiting when they saw a young boy coming. He had on a police cap that was too large for him and an old blue coat. He had his cornet in a small, dirty bag under his arm. Ridgley wondered what he was going to do as he walked over to meet young Louis Armstrong and have a little talk with him.

Ridgley explained that as the club members would have a little beer, they would request numbers for the band to play. Those tunes could be popular ones that even a beginner would know, but they could request all kinds of songs, like "Old Kentucky." Every time Ridgley asked about a particular tune, Louis said that he could play it, and Ridgley began to feel better. By the end of the weekend, Ridgley realized Louis could play more tunes than the rest of the band, and after that he was always glad to have Louis whenever he was short a cornet player. Ridgley's admiration for Louis shows through in the following reference.

> *Louis was a devilish little boy. When Louis was playing with the men in the Tuxedo Brass Band, if they were playing a funeral or something like that in the rough part of town the bad boys would follow Louis up, get right by him, call him everything you could think of, tell him "cause you're playing with the Tuxedo Band you think you're somebody." Louis would run them off down the street, for about half a block. Louis used to dance, shadow-box, everything. You couldn't learn what Louis learned as quick as he did; it had to be given to you by God. Louis got that from his birth. When he went on the boat, he could just spell a little, he couldn't read much, but with that wonderful ear of his, he could play third cornet; he was that good. Louis Armstrong was never a regular member of the band, but he jobbed around with them, sometimes in Celestin's place. He was young, very young; he hadn't started playing with no bands hardly yet.*

Amos White says Celestin and the band taught Armstrong how to read music. Armstrong's 1936 autobiography names mellophonist David Jones and pianist Fate Marable as the men that taught him to read music.

Armstrong gave Celestin the nickname of "Papa." Until then, the band had called Celestin by his other nicknames of "Sonny," "Zost," "Dog" or "Nostrils."

By 1921, Armstrong was marching with the Tuxedo Brass Band on most of its jobs and would have considered himself a member. In July 1923, Armstrong received the letter asking him to come to Chicago to play with

Joe "King" Oliver. Author James Leslie tells the story in the *Metronome Year Book 1958*: "Louis came up to Celestin after playing a parade in Algiers with Celestin's Tuxedo Brass Band and said he had to leave. 'He told me he could get $75.' Celestin recounted, 'and I knew then I couldn't keep him.' Celestin wasn't sure if that was the pay for a week or a month."

Armstrong and his all black band came back to New Orleans in 1931 to play at Sheehan's Suburban Gardens. He wasn't able to bring his racially mixed All-Star Band to New Orleans until after the 1950s because segregation laws in the South wouldn't allow them to stand, let alone perform, together on any stage.

Chapter 7

The Tuxedo Brass Band

Dressed in salvaged blue police uniforms, dark shoes and the standard eight-point cap (now called the jazz band cap), the Tuxedo Brass Band was considered one of the best New Orleans marching brass bands throughout the early 1920s. Celestin had formed the band in 1911 when he left the Red Allen Brass Band of Algiers, Louisiana, crossed the river and organized his own band. He named it the Tuxedo Brass Band after the dance hall whose name he had also given to the Tuxedo Jazz Band.

While Ridgley and Celestin shared the authority in directing the six-piece jazz band or the fourteen-piece jazz orchestra, Celestin alone was in charge of managing and leading the Tuxedo Brass Band, which

Tuxedo Brass Band, circa 1920. *Standing, left to right*: Yank Johnson, Manuel Perez, Oscar Celestin, Ernest Trepagnier and Charlie Love. George Hooker is crouching. *Courtesy of the Hogan Jazz Archive, Tulane University.*

would march with a grand marshall and eight musicians. In 1925, when Manuel Perez disbanded the Onward Brass Band, most of his regular musicians joined the Tuxedo. For any given job, Celestin could choose from a sizeable group of musicians.

When the band marched, there was an order to the lineup of the men. If there were three trumpets, one would play all the time, and the other two would come in for solos. Peter Bocage explained the process in an interview with Ralph Collins and Richard Allen in 1959.

The leader stands to the right, in front of the snare drum, see? The cornet in the middle is the solo part and so is the one on the outside, the other solo player. Well, now, you see, you have 2 solo men. Well, one of those men got to be up all the time, see? For instance, if you was playing solo with me, like I start the band off, I'm the leader, all right? Well, I play down that—you play right along, but you rest a little while I'm playing, see, and when I get ready to rest, you come up, see, and give me a chance to rest, see? But the first man, he plays all the time, see, but he's playing the first part. It's much easier than the solo part, see? But the two solo men got to work at intervals, you see, to give each a chance to rest, you understand? That's the way they work it, see?

There were always at least two trombones in the band. The first and second trombones would play the entire time. Each would play a different note to make a chord in combination with the players on the bass and baritone horns. "Black Happy" Goldston explained, "They also had trombone solos. Sunny Henry and August Rousseau were good with trombone solos. When there were three trombones in the lead of a funeral march, they would play a duet, together, first and second trombones. The bass drum is the foundation of any band. You have to keep the bass drum going at all times to hold the band together. The bass drum keeps the beat during breaks."

When Christopher "Black Happy" Goldston joined the Tuxedo Brass Band as a snare drummer, the rest of the band included Louis "Kid Shots" Madison, Willie Pajeaud and Celestin (tp), Charles "Sunny" Henry and August Rousseau (tb), Lorenzo Tio Sr. (cl), Adolphe Alexander Sr. (bar-hrn) and Ernest "Ninesse" Trepagnier (b-d).

Trepagnier, who was a reader and an improvisational player, taught Goldston how to play the bass drum and used to say, "Happy, why don't you learn bass drum? You don't have to learn it. You know it by walking with me for so long."

William Ridgley, circa 1920, wearing brass band attire. *Courtesy of the Hogan Jazz Archive, Tulane University.*

Goldston was content to only have to carry the snare drum and not the much heavier and bulky bass, which was twenty-four inches across and had a six-inch cymbal attached on top. Trepagnier explained that he might get sick and couldn't play, "and they say a bass drum is more important to a band than a snare drum. It is possible to pick up any kind of a snare drummer, but you can't pick up any kind of a bass drummer."

Trepagnier told Goldston that maybe sometimes they could switch and play the other's drum. Goldston thought about it and decided that he should learn the bass. One Sunday, they were playing a parade together, and Trepagnier told Goldston to "go ahead and put the bass drum on" and to give him the snare. They worked "like a clock" together.

Trepagnier had carried the drum for so long that he had damaged his left leg where the drum constantly hit him as he walked. In the mid-1920s, he had an operation on the leg and stopped playing for a long time after that. Celestin asked Goldston to take over as the bass drummer, which he did until the band was hired for a particularly long and hot parade. Afterward, Goldston went to Celestin and told him he'd had enough and to get someone else to play the bass drum. Goldston went back to playing the snare drum, and Celestin hired "Little Jim" Mukes to play the bass drum. Celestin put Goldston in charge of showing Mukes the Tuxedo way of marching and playing, and soon Goldston and Mukes were the talk of the town.

Early brass bands like the Tuxedo, the Excelsior and the Onward were very active playing dances and parties, where their selection of tunes would be popular songs that were beginning to get jazzed. But in reality, the brass bands in the city were most often hired to provide music for funerals.

Sketchy sanitation in the area, the lack of effective antibiotics and the constant yellow fever epidemics that burdened the city until late in the 1920s worked together to keep the brass bands marching. There was so much work to go around that the most sought-after bands would occasionally overbook a time slot, and the leader would find he had to be in two places at once. Sometimes the leader of the overbooked band would hire another band and let them play the job, and sometimes it was a little more convoluted. "Black Happy" Goldston said, "When Red Allen would get a job, he'd hire another band, like the Tuxedo Brass Band, all except the trumpet player." Allen's band, with a hired trumpet player, would fulfill its obligation to be at one place, and Allen would take his trumpet and lead another band, call it his own for the event and be at the second location. This was as close to a "jump-up" band (the kind of band that didn't play together regularly) as it got during this time period.

Funerals with music started as a benefit to which a person would be entitled as part of their membership in one of the city's benevolent associations. The benevolent associations were formed to help all New Orleanians with their medical expenses and were much like a modern-day HMO. If a person joined and paid his dues regularly to maintain his membership, he was then entitled to the services of participating medical professionals at a reduced rate. It was a family plan with both parents and all children covered.

The funeral benefits included the cost of the band that played slow, traditional marches to accompany the grieving friends and family on their walk to the cemetery. The graveside service included hymns like "I Want to Go Where Jesus Is." As everyone left the cemetery, the band would play a faster march as the mourners walked to the repast, a New Orleans tradition that takes place at home or, usually, in a rented social hall where everyone gathers after the funeral to socialize and share food.

The band wore its usual dark suits, or black pants and a white shirt, with dark eight-point caps, instead of the common white top. Standard dress for the mourners was appropriately somber for the women and children and a dark suit with white shirt for the men. The music was traditional, not jazzed at all.

Tuxedo Brass Band at a funeral, 1952. *Courtesy of the Hogan Jazz Archive, Tulane University.*

Louis Cottrell Jr. played saxophone and clarinet with the Tuxedo Jazz Band in the late 1920s and explained the benevolent associations and funerals to Rick Carter in an interview for the Hogan Jazz Archives on March 14, 1978.

Jazz was growing in these places all the time. Oh, like you hear so much about the second-line. Like you see a band on the street, you have so many bar rooms, and that was a common occurrence when I was coming up as a boy. Practically all over New Orleans, somewhere in the day, you had a funeral with music. Now they call it a jazz funeral, but at that time period it was just a funeral with music. It wasn't considered a jazz funeral. The modern day umbrellas at a second line are new. Used to use an umbrella in the rain, or a "rainbow" umbrella, to keep the sun off you. Most every person in this part of the country, especially in New Orleans, belong to these different benevolent associations because at the time they had doctors and medicine. When they'd have a funeral, that was given to the deceased cause you'd have to be a member. And they had what they called passive members which your wife and children, if you belong to the organization, they were entitled to the doctors and medicine. I mean when I was coming up, people didn't believe in hospitals. No, they didn't believe in hospitals at all. Mostly, yes, you take care of yourself. With the doctors you had so many doctors, and the doctors, most of them belong to these different benevolent association. Some of these associations, they had 3 or 4 doctors, that you had a choice of going to either one that you want. And I mean very good doctors—beautiful doctors, doctors that trained, doctors that were trained even in France. Quite a few. That was the life among the blacks around here. Not only blacks, but the whites too. Because plenty of the whites were serviced by these doctors. So you take up until the Depression when it hit here in 1929 and 1930. Well, at least in a week's time, you have 3–4 funerals around in town where they had music. You had 4 or 5 of these marching bands around, see, I mean it's a different caliber of music than anything that they be playing around here now. It was much better, to be truthful. Than what they be doing now. They were paid. They were part of the benevolent association. The service, that's right. They would pay the band, that's right. A lot of guys they earned their livelihood playing in the brass band. Well, of course, the cost of living was so cheap at the time. That was something else. Because my father raised a family with a wife and 5 kids and that's all he did was play music. He played until he died in 1927. I was 16 at the time that he died and all through my life, that's all I've been is a musician. In the depression, music funerals got expensive and the associations were helping the widow with some money instead. In the 30's and 40's they didn't want to give jazz funerals to the prostitutes and hustler part of the public. The benevolent associations wanted to associate with more professionals.

In the 1960s, after the resurgence of interest in New Orleans jazz, the city's tourist industry used the local tradition of the funeral with music, which they renamed a "jazz funeral," as a part of their national and international campaign to lure more tourists to the area.

Bob French, leader and drummer for the Tuxedo Jazz Band, was not impressed with the state of the modern funeral with music. "They have people coming here and going to funerals like it's a free show. They act like it's a circus. It's disgusting. They carry Mardi Gras umbrellas, they have snakes wrapped around their necks, they dress inappropriately and dance around shakin' their asses and acting the fool. It's a funeral, people. Show some respect."

Chapter 8
Jazz Travels by Riverboat

With Storyville closed, many bands tried different avenues in their search for employment. Some went north to Chicago or St. Louis to try and find steady jobs in the nightclubs there, but most stayed in New Orleans. The Gulf Coast circuit was closer and could be easily reached for the usual one-night gig. Band managers tried to book a string of them in a realistic travel pattern. Travel was by car, train or boat. Scattered gigs did not provide the dependable kind of income a husband needed to support a family, and because of the segregation issue, finding a place to sleep, eat or even use a bathroom could be a challenge for a black band when it traveled. Many New Orleans musicians looked to the Mississippi River—specifically, the passenger terminal at the foot of Canal Street where the excursion steamboats owned by Captain John Streckfus would dock to take on and discharge passengers.

The Streckfus Steamboat Line, which had been called the Acme Packet Company until 1911, was based in St. Louis and provided the first steamers used solely for day, afternoon or evening trips. The Streckfus excursion steamers offered steady employment to musicians and were an important and very competitive source of jobs in the late teens and early 1920s. The riverboats also played a vital part in the spread of New Orleans music to a broader audience. From May through late summer, the boats were based in St Louis and would make trips to the ports in St. Paul, Minnesota; Davenport, Iowa; and Pittsburgh, Pennsylvania for extended stays. The day trips from each of these ports were a popular way to enjoy the river scenery, a fine meal and entertainment. There was a bandstand and large wooden dance floor, and passengers would spend their time dining and dancing while the steamboats paddled up and down the river. After Labor Day, as the weather began to turn colder, the steamers would work their way back down the Mississippi to the winter port of New Orleans. Fate Marable, a pianist from Kentucky, had been hired in 1907 to play on the original riverboat, the *J.S.*, named for Captain John Streckfus. When the larger SS *Sidney* was commissioned in 1911, Marable was leading the band and helping Captain Streckfus search for new talent. It was Marable who scouted and then organized the first band of New Orleans musicians for the Streckfus Line in 1918 as World War I was ending.

The band Marable put together consisted of Joe Howard (cnt, tu), Louis Armstrong (cnt), Ridgley (tb), Davy Jones (mello), Johnny St. Cyr (bj), John Porter (b-vln, tu), George Foster (b), Marable (ldr, p) and Warren "Baby" Dodds (p). The group spent the winter playing the excursions from the Port of New Orleans, and then in the spring of 1919, Dodds, Armstrong and Ridgley stayed with Marable's band as the *Sidney* steamed off to the north for the summer season. Celestin remained in New Orleans to lead and manage both the Tuxedo Jazz Band and the Tuxedo Brass Band

Musicians on the Streckfus steamers were paid thirty-five dollars each week and had their room and board provided. If the boat was stationary in one port city and the musician found a room to rent in the black section of town, the wage was raised to sixty-five dollars, but they gave up their room and meals on board. The bandleader got an extra ten or fifteen dollars a week. For this salary, the band played the afternoon excursion and then the evening excursion. Captain Streckfus, a musician himself, demanded a two-hour practice session daily. His biggest concern was making sure the band maintained the proper tempo for dancing.

Dodds and Armstrong stayed with Marable, but after a month, Ridgley took his trombone and returned home. It had been the longest he was ever away from New Orleans. While being homesick may have played a part in his decision, he insisted he returned because he could make more money at home.

In New Orleans, Ridgley resumed his job as manager of the Tuxedo Jazz Band and looked up his friend Jack Sheehan, who offered the band a job at the Suburban Gardens. It started playing a regular gig there with Celestin (ldr, tp), Ridgley (tb), Edward Thoumy (cl), Willie Bontemps (g, bj), Tom Benton (g), Emma Barrett (p) and Henry Zeno or Arthur "Zutty" Singleton (d). Thoumy was with them for a time but left and was replaced by Paul "Polo" Barnes. The band didn't have anyone playing saxophone at the time.

Singleton was considered a member of the band even though he would only take "spot jobs." Zeno was the regular drummer until he died around 1918.

Amos White, another cornet player, met Celestin when he was hired by Ridgley in 1919 to play in the band at the Surburban Gardens. He wasn't from New Orleans, but he could read music and said, "The time I spent with the Tuxedo band helped me get the hang of New Orleans music eventually."

The band only had the job until January 17, 1920, the day Prohibition became law in the United States. The Suburban Gardens closed to the general public but didn't close its doors completely. Private parties that were under the radar of law enforcement continued to be held there, and the usual bands continued to be hired.

With the Suburban Gardens officially closed, the band needed to book more private jobs. It had a standing gig at the exclusive Boston Club and frequently played functions at Antoine's Restaurant, the Southern Yacht Club and the New Orleans Country Club. In November, with the start of debutante season, Ridgley continued to search the newspapers and send business cards to the parents.

David Hillyer interviewed a number of New Orleans residents in 1958. Elizabeth O'Kelly Kerrigan, born in 1905, told him, "I remember now that the first Negro jazz band that played at any social white parties in New Orleans was called the Tuxedo band, and Celestin was not the leader, but he was a member of the band. They played private parties and they might have played at the Country Club. I would say around 1918 or 1919."

Mary Lucy Hamill O'Kelly, another up-town woman, was interviewed and had these thoughts:

I can't remember when I first knew jazz as being jazz. I just thought it was sort of embroidery that the Negroes put on tunes that they played. They were not invented as jazz tunes, except for one I remember was the "St Louis Blues." These Negro bands would take any regular tune and jazz it up, they'd add little extra notes and quivers and trill and runs and syncopation and make the thing sound entirely different. For a long time we just thought it was something they took to naturally, because I never heard any Negro sing a tune exactly as it was written by white people. All the children thought it was wonderful. I thought all this jazz was dreadful, and I still do. But there's one good thing about it. It's wonderful to dance by, because the New Orleans bands keep such perfect time and with the jazz and they're not wandering off from hither and yonder.

School dances, a very popular form of weekly entertainment, would net thirty-six dollars for the band, with five dollars per musician and one dollar leftover, which Celestin and Ridgley would split as the leaders' bonus. Charles L. "Pie" Dufour, a New Orleans newspaper journalist, told Hillyer, "In high school, I would say what was played in those days was mainly what we called, and is still called, ragtime. I can remember the Tuxedo Band was a famous band, and they played what was genuinely called ragtime all the way down until I think about the '20s. That's when the saying 'jazz' came into the picture."

John G. Curran told Hillyer, "The first dance I went to was Oscar Celestin and the Dixieland band, in about 1923. I guess everybody in New Orleans was just crazy about Dixieland music. At that time in the '20s, it was primarily for dancing."

The Tuxedo Jazz Band played for the Twelfth Night Revelers at the Athenaeum every year on January 6 to celebrate the start of carnival season. All through the season, the band was in demand for different carnival balls. The Thursday before Mardi Gras, it would be back with the Twelfth Night Revelers for their ball and then with them again all day and night on Lundi Gras, the Monday before Mardi Gras. On Mardi Gras day, the Tuesday before Ash Wednesday, the band would play all day and night at the Boston Club. The pay was fifteen dollars per musician for each event, with the bandleaders each getting twenty-five dollars, a large amount of money for the time period.

John Curran talked about the popularity and size of the band with Hillyer.

And where their band has always been limited to seven, eight or possibly ten pieces, they might not play for the particular carnival ball, but the father or the grandfather will have that band playing in back for the maskers as they're dressing before the ball, and as they're taking their costumes off after the ball is over, and they're preparing to go in their full vest to the Queen's Supper. Occasionally they would go to the Queens's Supper, but as a general rule, they would have a much larger band, which they would have at the ball play at the Queen's Supper. They wouldn't hire New Orleans jazz bands at the balls because they wouldn't have the number of pieces in it. A Dixieland band just cannot play with more than nine pieces. Large bands, of up to thirty pieces, if they would play a Dixieland number, they'll immediately cut it down to seven to ten pieces. Today, I would say that during the month of May, right at this time, I keep referring to Celestin's band because he did have a band as far back as 1904, and his band is still going today, with the exception of Celestin, who passed away several years ago, there's been no substitution in his band, and today you couldn't hire that band through the month of December, he's just closed up completely. And the very few times from the time the debutante season opened would he have open engagement, right on through till Mardi Gras. That's applying right now, with Mardi Gras nine months away.

Evelyn Sinclaire Moyer gave Hillyer her opinions.

In the 1920s and '30s, debuts were given at the Patio Royal and a few at the Orlean Club and of course some in people's homes. But for the most part, most of them were given at the Patio Royal. There were a few given at the Roosevelt Roof and a few at the Country Club. We certainly did have jazz bands at them. With Dixieland jazz I don't think we would have gone and sat and listened to Dixieland Jazz like you all do today. I don't ever remember doing that in the late '20s and early '30s. You had a Dixieland jazz band to dance to, but you didn't stand around and listen to it. And you didn't go anywhere and listen to it. It was more to dance by, than it was to listen to. And in my day, people danced, they didn't sit.

Jack Kerrigan also spoke with Hillyer.

Until 1926 or '27 all debutante parties, the Country Club, the St Charles Hotel and the Gold room, were spots used to give the debutante parties, also the Roosevelt Hotel and private homes requested and used jazz bands at approximately 98 percent of the parties given. At the present time [1958] we are still using Celestin's band, which was one of the outstanding colored bands in the later years of jazz in the city of New Orleans.

A chance encounter could lead to work. Charles "Pie" Dufour, a writer for the *State's Item*, related a story from the early 1920s when he and some friends hired "Papa" Celestin's band to serenade the dean of the School of Law at Tulane. Dufour and his friend and fellow law student Hamilton Basso had been labeled troublemakers by Dean Judd Northrup and were already being encouraged to go elsewhere for their education.

It all happened as four or five of us headed up St. Charles Avenue from Gibson Hall for the drugstore on Broadway and St. Charles. It was between classes.

As we ambled along, we spotted on the other side of the avenue a truck with four or five musicians in it. "Tuxedo Band" read a sign on the truck. It happened in a jiffy. An idea sprang fully matured from some idle brain. Basso's or mine. I don't recall which.

"Hey, wait a minute," we yelled to the musicians, and the truck pulled to a stop in front of Audubon Park. A hasty survey of finances ensued as we walked across to the truck.

"We'll give you two dollars if you'll play one tune for us," we said.

"What tune do you want?" asked Papa as the musicians started tuning up.

"Oh, not here," we explained. "We want you to come over to Tulane and serenade our dean."

And so, Papa Celestin and his musicians, a few moments later, climbed out of their truck and set up shop under Dean Northrup's window. I'm ashamed to tell the tune we asked for, "I'll Be Glad When You're Dead You Rascal You."

Soon after that, he found himself out of school and a full-time newspaperman.

Chapter 9
The Band, Baseball and Texas

T he first jazz bands were usually six instruments, with the front line being the trumpet, trombone and clarinet. Behind them on the bandstand would be a guitar or banjo, piano and drums. Vocals were handled by the existing musicians, but an occasional guest vocalist might be hired to join them.

In the mid-1920s, saxophones were added to the front line and sousaphones to the rhythm section. The clarinet, with its softer tone, was starting to lose favor as the bands went for a sharper, brassier sound. Celestin added extra brass as needed, but he didn't eliminate the clarinet. He continued leading the brass band and the jazz band, which would be referred to as the Tuxedo Jazz Orchestra when there were eleven or more musicians. In the later 1920s, the orchestras were shifting to as many as fourteen players.

With the ability to configure the band as needed, Celestin and Ridgley were able to book many different types of jobs. They continued to pick up work where they could, which wasn't always in the usual nightclub, restaurant or private home. In 1923, Commodore Jahncke hired Celestin's band to play on his private yacht, *Reveille*, for a trip across Lake Pontchartrain from New Orleans to Madisonville. A private motion picture was made of the trip, according to drummer Abby "Chinee" Foster. The weather was stormy, and the band members were warned not to go, but they made the cruise without incident.

When Piron took his band to New York City for an extended engagement in 1923, the Tuxedo Orchestra was hired to take his place at Tranchina's Restaurant, a lively spot in the resort area of Spanish Fort on Lake Pontchartrain, where the dancing went until midnight. The Tuxedo Band

More than a Century of a New Orleans Icon

Tuxedo Jazz Band, June 1924. *Left to right:* James Willigan (d), Simon Marrero (b), John Marrero (bj), Eddie Cherrie (cl), Paul Barnes (sax), William Ridgley (tb) and Oscar Celestin (cnt). *Courtesy of the Hogan Jazz Archive, Tulane University.*

at that time consisted of Celestin (ldr, tp), Ridgley (tb), Eddie Cherrie (cl), Paul Barnes (sax), John Marrero (bj), Simon Marrero (b) and Abby "Chinee" Foster (d). Foster, who had replaced Zeno when he died, was now the band's regular drummer.

On June 13, 1924, the Gates Aerial Circus flew in from California for its yearly show on the lakefront. The Tuxedo was still playing at Tranchina's, and by virtue of being in the right place at the right time, it became one of the first bands to play in an airplane. The band members went up two at a time. Celestin (tp) and Ridgley (tb) went first, then Paul Barnes (sax) and John Marrero (bj) and then lastly, the combination of Eddie Cherrie (cl) and Simon Marrero (b). Sam Dutrey Sr., who had become the regular clarinet player, missed the ride because he was off that day. They played "Maryland, My Maryland" and, because it had been a very dry summer, "It Ain't Gonna Rain No More."

Celestin, in an interview with John Curran for the Hogan Jazz Archives, said, "That wind was strong up there, man, snatched the horn from my mouth."

From the early 1920s until about 1930, the Tuxedo Brass Band, led by Celestin, had a standing engagement at Heinemann Park (later re-named Pelican Stadium) on the downtown, riverside corner of Tulane Avenue and

Carrollton Avenue in New Orleans. When there was a Sunday home game for the New Orleans Pelicans baseball club, the band would be there by 10:00 a.m. to pump up the crowd's enthusiasm and keep them entertained between double headers

The band that played for the games was led by Celestin (tp) and included Ridgley (tb), Willard Thoumy (cl), Paul Barnes (sax), John Marrero (bj), "Cato" or Simon Marrero (b) and Abby Foster (d).

Charles L. "Pie" Dufour talked with David Hillyer about going to baseball games at Heinemann Park.

> At the ball park for example, in the old days, the baseball park, I remember going back in 1926–27 and every Sunday at the double-header, they'd have a band in the Negro bleachers, and they'd play that "Maryland" roll call, and man they'd make the crowd go crazy. Everyone, even the white people loved it. And every time the Pelicans went on a rally or Pelicans came to bat, they'd give a couple of these fan fares and go off into it. That used to be a regular feature on some of those when you had 8, 10 or 12 thousand people on a Sunday. That was the great days of the 20's as from 23-30. They played what was hot for the day. They played "Jada, Jada, Jing, Jing, Jing," "Pretty Baby," that sort of stuff. Twenty years earlier they were playing "I Wonder Who's Kissing Her Now?" which would be waltzing. The thing was pepped up and "jazzed up" as the expression went.

The Pelicans played professional baseball in the double-A, minor Dixie League with which the Southern Association was affiliated. The team's goal each year was to win the Southern Association pennant and go to the Dixie Series, which was held in different cities around the south. In 1923, the Pelicans won their fifth Southern Association pennant and took the Tuxedo Band with them to Fort Worth, Texas, where they lost the Dixie Series to the Fort Worth team. In Fort Worth, the band set up a bandstand on the back of a truck in the downtown business district near city hall. There were so many city employees hanging from the windows and dancing in the building that the mayor closed the city offices for the rest of the day so the employees could officially stop working and go outside to listen and dance.

In Texas, the audiences went wild over a technique Abby Foster used where he blew or talked into his snare drum to get another musical effect. In a 1960 interview for the Hogan Archives, Foster described the technique he used when singing into his snare. He stood and kept the beat going on his bass drum while tightening or loosening the snares with his right hand to coincide with the pitch of the animal sounds he made as he blew or sang across the drumhead, snare side. In "Tiger Rag" and "Livery Stable Blues," he would imitate the various animals by roaring across the drumhead. He said Punch Miller and he invented the idea in 1919.

Abby Foster remembers, "Celestin's band won a competition at the Southern Yacht Club against James Williams 'Red Happy' Bolton playing with John Robecheaux's band, by his blowing across his drums. The band won the cup. Red Happy always played his own way, and I played for the band."

In the early fall of 1926, the Pelicans won their sixth Southern Association pennant, and the Tuxedo Band traveled to Texas with them again as they tried to win the Dixie Series, but they lost to the Dallas team in Dallas. The band had a chance to play several charity jobs while there, including a Milk Fund Drive in Dallas, where they were joined by the Police Band of New Orleans. The ladies in Texas that were organizing the event and hoping to raise $25,000 for the milk fund were thrilled when Celestin told them he wouldn't charge for the half hour they were going to play.

Chapter 10

The First Recordings

1925

In 1917 in New York City, a New Orleans band, the Original Dixieland Jazz Band led by Nick LaRocca, recorded the "Livery Stable Blues" for Victor records. It was a sensation, and because of the band's name, people began to refer to the music coming out of New Orleans as "Dixieland." Willie "Bunk" Johnson called it ragtime.

Louis Cottrell explained how the Original Dixieland Band was chosen for the first jazz recording in 1917.

> *Creole Jazz Band was the first of that type of music* [that] *left New Orleans. In the teens, thirteen, they went on the Orpheum Circuit. And they traveled and stuff and that's how it began moving around.* [Freddy] *Keppard was approached first to record, but he said no, he didn't want to because they would steal what he knew. The Original Dixieland Band, which was white, they grabbed the chance of it in 1917, and now they were the first band from down this way to record any jazz music. Most of the things they recorded was things that these fellows had been playing and had already gotten. They went on to record it and plenty of them got the credit for it. Because, we have to face it, our folks were limited to a certain extent. They didn't get copyright on the things, also they lost out on plenty of numbers, which they got credit for it as being the first ones. And that's all you going to hear too because afterwards they didn't have others to follow through behind it right them. Like whites, blacks was just following one another. You see, because you had Keppard and after Keppard you had* [Joe] *Oliver and after Oliver you had* [Louis] *Armstrong and I mean it*

kept moving around. Which with the others after Dixieland it took a long time. They'd sit around, the Royal Garden at the time, that's why this song that you hear, I don't know if you know it or not, called the "Royal Garden Blues." Well, that was made up by them. In the latter part of the '20s and '30s that's when they began to branch out. The Original Dixieland Band recorded and got the credit cause they were the first to record it.

Interest in the new form of music was growing, and in 1925, the Okeh Record Company, an independent record label founded in 1918 by German American Otto K.E. Heinemann, brought its mobile recording equipment to New Orleans. The label traveled throughout the South recording indigenous musicians, and on January 23, 1925, Celestin's Original Tuxedo Jazz Orchestra was recorded at Spanish Fort.

The band members listed on the recording were Celestin (cnt), Louis "Shots" Madison (tp), Ridgley (tb), Willard Thoumy (cl, as), John Marrero (bj), Simon Marrero (b), Manuel Manetta (p) and Abby Foster (d, swannee whistle).

The swannee whistle, also called a slide whistle, has a mouthpiece like a recorder with a tubular body outfitted with a piston that is slid in and out to vary the pitch. They were most common in the 1920s and are infrequently used today. Foster had been playing the slide whistle since the early 1920s after he got the idea from Louis Armstrong when they were playing on the boat.

Manetta says he was the piano player on the Okeh session at Ridgley's request. Ridgley confirms this. Foster also named Manetta as the piano player, not Emma Barrett.

Foster said that there was another lineup that recorded all three of those songs. He names: Celestin (first tp), "Shots" Madison (second tp), Ridgley (tb), Sidney Carriere (sax), Percy Prejaud (ts), Paul Barnes (as), John Marrero (bj), Simon Marrero (b), Manuel Manetta (p) and Abby Foster (d).

The three songs recorded were "Careless Love," "The Original Tuxedo Rag"—both written by Celestin—and "The Black Rag," written by Ridgely. Recorded but not released was a song named "High Society" or "Hoye Nellie."

"The Black Rag" was originally called "Down Home Rag," but the record company suggested the name change, probably to avoid paying for the use. It was not uncommon for a band to cover up or tear off the title from their sheet music in an attempt to keep other musicians from using the same tune. When it came time to record, the musicians would rename and take credit for the tune. The reasoning was that they had created their own cover version of it.

The recording equipment used by Okeh in 1925 was the same as the original acoustic process invented by Thomas Edison in 1877. Sound entered the large bell end of a horn and traveled to a diaphragm at the short end. The sound waves vibrated the diaphragm, which moved a stylus that cut a groove into a prepared cylinder or disc coated with wax. This method worked well with individual voices, but when there was an entire band being recorded, the acoustic method couldn't cover the frequency range needed to accurately reproduce the sound.

"The recording equipment would not pick up the bass drum, but Foster was playing it anyway," Paul Barnes said about Ridgley's "Original Tuxedo Rag." He also said that on "Careless Love," there "weren't too many solos because bands played that way then and that the trumpet players took down their horn to dry their lips only."

Chapter 11

The Ridgley-Celestin Split

A few months later, in the fall of 1925, Ridgley and Celestin split, and according to Ridgley, there was some knavery involved. On that Wednesday night the Tuxedo Jazz Band played its regularly scheduled dance at the Pythian Temple's Parisian Roof Garden. Built in 1908 at the corner of Gravier and Saratoga Streets (now Loyola Avenue), the Pythian Temple was an upscale venue owned by blacks, where middle- and upper-class blacks gathered to listen and dance to popular jazz bands. The cost of admission in November of 1925 was fifty cents to enter the ground-level Pythian Temple and another thirty cents to go up to the Parisian Roof Garden.

After the gig, in the wee hours of Thursday morning, Celestin, John Marrero and his brother Simon were having drinks together and decided they would be better off if they split with Ridgley. They made plans to go to the president of the Southern Yacht Club, a Mr. Garcia, and tell him that Ridgley had quit playing music and was turning the Tuxedo Jazz Orchestra over completely to Celestin.

"Shots" Madison, another trumpet player in the band who was sitting close by, overheard the conversation and called Ridgley at about 4:00 a.m. to give him a heads-up.

When Ridgley got to the Southern Yacht Club at about 11:00 that morning, Garcia wanted to know why he was there. Ridgley told him he had "heard something blowing in the wind and had come down to talk about it."

Garcia asked if Ridgley had quit playing music. Ridgley replied that he had not quit playing and wanted to know who said he had.

Pythian Temple Roof Garden, 1923. *Courtesy of the Hogan Jazz Archive, Tulane University.*

Garcia said Celestin had come by early that morning, and the Southern Yacht Club had drawn up a contract with Celestin's band. He described Celestin as "that heavyset, dark fellow…used to smoke those cigarettes and go out on the porch all the time."

Garcia and Ridgley sorted out what had happened, then Garcia asked Ridgley how many of the original band members did he still have to work with.

Ridgley said, "The girl, Emma Barrett, a drummer and five others."

Garcia told him to come out for the regular gig with whomever he had, and then he called in a stenographer and had her write Celestin a letter telling him that different arrangements had been made with another band and that he would not be needed.

Ridgley pulled together a group of musicians and called his new band Ridgley's Original Tuxedo Jazz Band. The band was already booked for the weekly job at the Southern Yacht Club, and it took no time at all for Ridgley to approach his long list of contacts for work. As manager of the Original Tuxedo Band, the switch to doing business as Ridgley's Original Tuxedo Band was easy. He answered the same phone as before and did his regular

Old Southern Yacht Club. *Courtesy of the New Orleans Jazz Club Collection of the Louisiana State Museum.*

job as manager. People knew Celestin, but it was Ridgley they had done business with.

The band Ridgley pulled together had Madison (tp), Ridgley (tb), Willie "Kaiser" Joseph (sax, cl), Robert Hall (ts), Arthur Derbigny and Cecil Thornton (sax), Willie Bontemps (bj, voc), Emma Barrett—who he nicknamed "Eyes" (p)—and Nathaniel "Bebe" Matthews (d).

Ridgley said in an interview for the Hogan Jazz Archives in 1961 that the people who hired the new band and the people who listened and danced to their music told him they couldn't tell the difference between the present and the previous band. But he could.

Ridgley's unusually strict rules for the band helped him schedule first-class work for it. The band continued to get a lot of society work because people loved the way the members carried themselves. He felt they were being paid a salary to play music, so that was what they were expected to do. The musicians couldn't leave their positions on the bandstand until the entire band took its scheduled break. There was no smoking while working.

No drinking was allowed at any time on the bandstand or on any break that included food. If the musicians were given liquor at the intermission, they could take it home but they couldn't drink it there.

It was common, though not mandatory, for bands to have food provided for them as soon as they arrived on the job or at the break. If Ridgley's men came on the job expecting to eat first, he told them they knew they were coming to work so they should have eaten before they got there, and he knew they wouldn't starve in a couple of hours. Some band members didn't like his rules, but they were making good money so they didn't leave.

The band also played advertising jobs. One of its weekly jobs was to play for two hours inside a department store on Canal Street.

Ridgley booked his Original Tuxedo Band to play the opening night at the Pelican Club, at 301 South Rampart Street. Located on the corner of Gravier and South Rampart Streets, the Pelican was one short block from the popular Parisian Roof Garden. The club was in the same building as the Astoria Hotel and was managed by A.J. Fabacher. Both the Pelican and the Astoria were listed in the New Orleans City Guide Book put out by the Federal Writer's Project for the Works Progress Administration (WPA) in 1930 as being "negro restaurants." A table d'hôte lunch at either place cost $0.15 to $0.35, and dinner was $0.20 to $0.40. Over at 123 Barrone Street in the Fountain Room at the Roosevelt, where only whites could be served, a table d'hôte lunch was $0.45 to $1.50. Coffee and donuts at the French Market Coffee Stands would put you back ten cents—but were only available to whites.

After its successful opening night, Ridgley's band was hired for a regular gig in the elegantly appointed two-story auditorium. The 1920s were well known as a time for drinking, dancing and flamboyant parties, and the Pelican Club provided all of that. Well-dressed, well-heeled couples would fill the club for a night of socializing and dancing to the best jazz in the city.

Every band in New Orleans, either local or passing through, would at some point be at the Pelican to take on another band in a "cutting" contest: a musical sparring contest between bands as a form of entertainment. The nightclub would organize the contests, charge admission, hire the judges and flood the city with advertising.

Ridgley knew he had put together a good band, and he wanted the people to know who had the best band between the two Tuxedo Bands, so he and Celestin drew up a contest to be held at the Pelican. Celestin knew his band was the best and no doubt also expected to win. The Pelican management put placards up around the city and placed advertisements in the newspaper about the two Tuxedo Jazz Bands that were going to "buck." Davy Jones wrote to a music house in New York and had them send two complete sets of the sheet music for the two numbers chosen for the competition— "By the Waters of the Minnetonka" and "Louisiana Bo Bo." The bands rehearsed those numbers and also chose the other tunes they would play in the competition.

Celestin decided to go with "Maryland, My Maryland" and "My Josephine," his two most popular numbers when he played with "Shots" Madison. But now Ridgley had "Shots," and he wanted to slip those two songs in before Celestin had a chance to play them.

The night of the competition, the man who did the booking for Loew's State Theatre, always looking to keep up with the local scene, was there to assess the talent. John Robichaux, A.J. Piron and Dave Perkins were the judges hired by the Pelican Club. The club itself was packed to overflowing, and there were cars filled with rich white jazz lovers parked around the building that housed the black club, hoping to hear the bands play.

Ridgley's band set up on a bandstand at one end of the room. He had with him his usual band: "Shots" Madison (tp), Ridgley (tb), Joe Watson

Ridgley's Tuxedo Jazz Band, 1926. *Left to right:* Nathaniel Matthews (d), William Ridgley (tb), Louis Terman (tp), Willie Joseph (sax), Emma Barrett (p), Arthur Derbigny (sax), Cecil Thornton (sax), Jessie [last name unknown] (tu), Robert Hall (ts) and Willie Bontemps (bj). *Courtesy of the New Orleans Jazz Club Collection of the Louisiana State Museum.*

(cl), Robert Hall (ts), Davy Jones (sax, mello), John Porter (souse), Willie Bontemps (bj), Emma Barrett (p) and Goldston (d).

Celestin's band, with Celestin and Ricard Alexis (tp), August Rousseau and Bill Matthews (tb), Barnes (as), Sidney Carriere (ts), Simon Marrero (tu), John Marrero (bj), Jeanette Salvant (p) and Abby Foster (d), took to the bandstand on the other end of the ballroom.

"Black Happy" Goldston recalls, "Ridgley started with the two great big heavy numbers then they played 'Josephine' and then 'Maryland.' Celestin followed with the same selections. The crowd and the judges all went with declaring Ridgley's Original Tuxedo Band the winner."

That same night, Celestin approached Goldston and asked if he wanted to join with Celestin's band, but Goldston told him that he was happy where he was. Celestin told Goldston negative things about Ridgley to try to persuade him to change his mind and leave Ridgley's band, but Goldston insisted that Ridgley had never done anything to him and he liked his job with the band. Celestin kept the conversation going until Goldston finally promised him that if he should ever quit Ridgley, he would join his Tuxedo.

Celestin wouldn't let it rest and kept after him with constant reminders of his offer. He had his chance on a night when the Tuxedo was playing a job close to Goldston's home. When Foster got drunk and didn't show up for work, Celestin sent someone to get Goldston, who came and played the job with them. The whole band ganged up on Goldston and tried to get him to continue playing with them. Finally, they wore him down, and he started drumming regularly with Celestin and then stayed with him for twenty-eight years.

John G. Curran describes a contest on the SS *Cincinnati*, which was recommissioned as the SS *President* in 1934.

> Back in the '20s, they would have a contest between two Dixieland bands, and they would offer some prize or a loving cup for the band that had the greatest applause. They had a cash prize on the steamer President, and Jan Garber's band was at one end of the President and Oscar "Papa" Celestin's band was at the other end and they asked to have Garber play first. Celestin's band decided that regardless of what number Garber played, they would play it right back again. After Garber heard them play it back, the first time he played which was "High Society," he walked over to Celestin's band and put out his hand.

Bands would not only be hired to play in established clubs but also in "pop-up" halls. On Clio Street, the Gypsy Camp had been set up with a tent

Oscar Celestin with trophies from cutting contests, circa 1930s. *Courtesy of the New Orleans Jazz Club Collection of the Louisiana State Museum.*

and was being used for a church meeting during the days but was available in the evening. A group of white boys rented it for the night to have a dance and used a cutting contest as an extra incentive to fill the place. The boys hired Ridgley's band and Henry "Kid" Rena's band, and when it was over, Ridgley's band had won that contest.

There were cutting contests at the Bulls Club, located at Eighth and Rampart Streets, every Tuesday night. The National Park, located at Third and Willow Streets, was another popular location for cutting contests. Ridgley's Tuxedo went up against Jack Carey's band there and came out the winner.

Ridgley said his band "whipped" Edward "Kid" Ory's band at the Turtles parade. The Turtles were an organization of one thousand or so black men who laid all the sewer lines in the city. That same night, the Turtles gave a dance at the National Park, and Ridgley's band beat out Kid Ory's band again. Unfortunately for the Turtles, one of their own men stole all the admission money during the dance and ran off with it.

Ridgley said that in all, he got three medals for the contests. He gave one to a friend, one to his brother and kept one for himself. He wasn't sure if they won because they had the best band or because they had such a good name.

Ridgley had another group of musicians he played with in a band he named the Black Diamond: Bat Brown (tp), "Shots" Madison (tp), Ridgley (tb), Joe Watkins (cl, sax), Paul Barnes (as), "Big Head" Eddie Johnson (ts), Cecil Thornton from St. Louis (sax) and "Black Happy" Goldston (d). They got a copy of the Louis Armstrong and His Hot Five record that was released by Okeh in November 1925, learned all the songs and then got themselves booked for a cutting contest at the Pelican. The bands were supposed to play one song at a time and take turns, but the Black Diamond played straight through the entire record, whipped the crowd into a frenzy and won the contest hands down.

Other musicians played with Ridgley's Original Tuxedo Jazz Band at various times over the years. Gilbert Young started playing trumpet with Ridgley when he was quite young and advanced to playing second cornet. Ridgley said of him, "I taken him when he tried to read and he couldn't play four quarters in a bar…He got so his head got so big I had to get rid of him. Had a good tone and good ragtime in his head."

Ridgley also spoke about Earl Fouche, who played saxophone with Ridgley starting in 1927 for a few years. "He's another fellow got a big head…You couldn't get along with him. Thought he was the only sax player in town."

George McCullum, Arnold Metoyer and Adolphe "Tats" Alexander Jr. all took a turn playing cornet. Ricard Alexis played the trumpet and bass with Ridgley until, as Ridgley put it, "When he got to drinking, he wouldn't listen, he'd get contrary and you couldn't tell him nothing."

Willie Bontemps played banjo and, as Ridgley said, "would sing a plenty." Some of the men Ridgley listed as playing "spot jobs" were: Davey Jones (sax, mello), August Rousseau (tb), Jimmy Johnson (b), Joe Harris (as), Alex "Rock" Scott (sax), Sam Dutrey Jr. (sax, cl), Louis Cottrell (sax, cl) and Emmanuel Sayles (bj, g).

By the early 1930s, Ridgley had developed pyorrhea, a painful infection of the gums that can cause severe tissue and even bone destruction, and the discomfort he experienced while playing the trombone led him to switch to playing drums. He gave up on that idea almost immediately when he decided he really didn't like drumming. He tried to keep a steady trombone player as his replacement but couldn't. Then he became acquainted with a man named "Red" who played the trombone and was in New Orleans every year with the circus. Ridgley asked him if he'd want to take his place in the band as the trombone player. Red seemed to like the idea but told Ridgley he had to go to Tulsa, Oklahoma, where the circus would disband, and he would write to Ridgley when he got there. Ridgley gave him all his sheet music to study, and when Red got to Tulsa, he wrote to Ridgley with some interest in the job. Ridgley told him to come back to New Orleans and take his place with the band.

When Red got back to New Orleans, he complained to Ridgley that his horn was "kind of bad," so Ridgley let him use his. Red offered to buy it, and Ridgley said he "sold it to him for $25.00 although he had paid either $192.00 or $192.50 for it." Red gave Ridgley $5.00, and that was the last Ridgley ever saw of Red.

Ridgley struggled with leading the band until 1936, when he dissolved it after surviving a stroke that left him partially paralyzed. He blamed his poor health on living the life of a musician. He joined the church and stopped playing altogether.

In 1958, Samuel B. Charters found him "living with his daughter and her family, selling peanuts on the street car stop at the corner of Carrollton Avenue and Claiborne Avenue. He walks with a slight dragging of the right leg, but he is able to get around and is quite active in his church."

As Ridgley said, "I been everything in the church but the preacher, and I didn't try to be that because I wasn't learnt enough for that."

Chapter 12

Celestin and the American Federation of Musicians Local 496, Colored

While the two competing bandleaders were both laying claim to a jazz orchestra with the name of Tuxedo, Celestin continued to lead the Tuxedo Brass Band, which he had founded back in 1911. Oddly enough, Ridgley continued to occasionally play trombone in that band.

Celestin remembered that a woman approached him in either 1927 or 1928, when the Tuxedo Brass Band was playing a funeral in Gretna, and asked if he could learn a new song. He went behind a tombstone with her and she sang the song for him until he got it. The song was "When the Saints Go Marching In." A version of this song had been recorded as early as 1924 by the Payne-Elkins Jubilee Singers as sacred music. But most locals believed John G. Curran when he said, "'When the Saints Go Marching In' ['The Saints'] was played for the first time by Oscar Celestin, which was in 1927. And he failed to copyright it."

After the Celestin/Ridgley split, Celestin reorganized his Tuxedo Jazz Band to include Celestin (ct), Ricard Alexis (second ct), August Rousseau (tb), Paul Barnes (as), Sid Carriere (ts), Simon Marrero (tu), John Marrero (bj), Jeanette Salvant (p) and Clifford "Snags" Jones (d) for a short time until he was replaced by Foster, who became the regular drummer. Adolph Alexander (ct, bar-hrn) worked with the band and did a lot of its arrangements until about 1931.

Jeanette Salvant Kimball confirmed this was the configuration of the band for about 2 years. The band played mostly stock arrangements at society jobs all around the city of New Orleans. She had been hired by Celestin immediately after graduating high school in 1926 and played her first musical date with him at the Pythian Temple's Parisian Roof Garden. On September 19, 1926, she was with Celestin when the band played for the New Orleans University Senior Prom. She rarely traveled and was with the big band, the fourteen-piece orchestra, until 1935.

Bob French has said, "She was the only person that pronounced Papa's name as Ce-LES-tin. Everyone else pronounced it, CEL-es-tin."

Mercedes "Candy" Fields or Lee Sherie Tucker would occasionally fill in for Jeanette Kimball locally or when the band traveled.

The nightclubs around the city were busy and were always a good place to go for work, but the best place for a steady job was still on a Streckfus steamer, where the thirty-five dollars a week plus room and board was a better deal than before. The pay was the same as before, but the work was halved. Captain Streckfus was now hiring at least two bands in each port. One would play for the afternoon dance, and another was the entertainment for the evening excursion.

Musicians who stayed land-bound had to hustle to get jobs, and unless the job was in New Orleans, there were travel expenses involved. In the early 1920s, jobs paid five dollars and up per musician. The union wasn't very active.

The only way to be hired for one of the union jobs offered by Captain Streckfus was to go through the American Federation of Musicians (AFM). There were white AFM Locals in most cities, and some larger cites, such as St. Louis, also had black Locals. New Orleans had the white Local No. 174, which had been established in February 1902. The black Local No. 242 was organized later that year, and the August 31, 1902 *New Orleans Item* announced that Theogene V. Baquet (leader of the Excelsior Brass Band) had been named president, James MacNeal the vice-president, Wendell MacNeal the financial secretary, Nelson J. Jean the recording secretary and William Cornish the sergeant-at-arms. By November 1905, Local No. 242 was no longer active and had been stricken from the list of Locals.

In the 1920s, you needed a union card to be hired by the steamship lines. Fate Marable's band was based in St. Louis, which had a black Local where musicians were able to apply for and sign contracts. This gave them an advantage over New Orleans musicians, who had to travel 150 miles to Mobile, Alabama, the site of the closest black Local. When the SS *Capitol* had been put in service in 1920, Celestin had been unable to get his band a job with Streckfus because he was, at that time, non-union.

When black New Orleans musicians were refused membership in the white Local No. 174 in New Orleans, Celestin was determined to form a chapter for

Riverboat *Capitol. Courtesy of the Hogan Jazz Archive, Tulane University.*

the black musicians in his city. He organized a group of black musicians who persisted until they were able to obtain a charter for Local No. 496, Colored, in 1926. In honor of his efforts, Celestin was elected the first president. He served his first term with secretary Osceola Blanchard and treasurer Peter Bocage. Alec Lanaville replaced Celestin around 1928 as president.

In 1926, with equal access to union jobs, Celestin was able to get the Original Tuxedo Jazz Orchestra hired to play on the SS *Capitol*, the flagship of the Streckfus lines since its launch in 1920. The band that Celestin had on the SS *Capitol* included Celestin (tp), Guy Kelly (tp), Bill Matthews (tb), Joe Rouzon and Clarence Hall (sax), Narvin Kimball (bj), Simon Marrero (b), Jeanette Salvant (p), Abby Foster (d) and Joe Thomas (voc).

As president of Local No. 496, Colored, Celestin would be called on whenever an issue arose between the two Locals, as in this excerpt taken directly from the minutes of the August 13, 1926 weekly meeting of the board of directors of Local No. 174, AFM.

> *H.* [H.C. Voorhees, board member] *I saw a circular yesterday that a negro brought into the store. A negro non-union band is hired to play a dance for the Central Trades and Labor Council. It's to be played at the Temple. It is a white outfit. A fellow came to me Wednesday to know if*

More than a Century of a New Orleans Icon

Celestin's Tuxedo Jazz Orchestra, circa 1926. *Left to right:* Bill Matthews, Guy Kelly, Oscar Celestin, Jeanette Salvant Kimball, Narvin Kimball, Joseph Thomas, Abby Foster, Simon Marrero, Joe Rouzon and Clarence Hall. *Courtesy of the Hogan Jazz Archive, Tulane University.*

he should join the Union. I said yes. He said what is the use when I can work on jobs without belonging to the Union. We have negroes working on white jobs and they are working below our scale.

A. [Albert A. Levy, president] *I think we should communicate with the National office and find out who are the officers of this colored local.*

H. Celestin is the president. How are we going to control that?

A. When we find out who the officers are we can write to the [National] *president* [Joseph Weber] *and investigate.*

H. I thought you could demand a duplicate.

Secretary: I informed you all of that. I also read the letter from [Secretary] *Kernwood which says we have a right to inquire into the prices they get.*

H. For Labor Day parades. I heard that these negroes are underbidding one another.

B. [Bob Aguilera, board member] *The building Trades is the only organization going out mixed. Some of these fellows went out and said the price was $55.00.*

A. We will have to write to the National office and find out who's in charge.

H. I am getting all the dope from my customers. There's a negro working at the Bungalow. This negro joined the union and he delivered a new contract to his boss at union scale and they threw him out.

B. They take out of town engagements and they are playing for about half of our price.

H. We could communicate with the Mobile Local and see what they are doing.

B. We could send a man over there.

H. We have to do something.

A. We wrote to one of our own members in Mobile asking for information and didn't get it.

B. The most it would cost would be $15.00. I think the information would be needed here. It only means one day. They could leave that evening.

A. The motion is that we send a representative to Mobile to call on the Secretary and get information from him as to how they handle the colored Local.

H. Let's spend a 2 cents stamp and write Mobile.

Secretary: We were told by Kernwood how to handle that. I asked him of the supervision we would have over the affairs with the colored Local. He says we would have supervision over them in so far as that we might ask for exact information and an affidavit on the price they receive when they play engagements, for all engagements, played for white folks. For their own race we have no look into it. Whenever we would find out there was a difference in the price between theirs and ours we would then notify Secretary Kernwood. My idea is this: if we were to send to the Mobile Local we would simply receive the very same answer and positively would show that we have very little imagination.

B. They have been experienced in handling that. I make a motion that a committee of one look up the President and Secretary in town and get them to give you the names of everybody in the Local.

A. I said we could write to Weber and get it officially.

B. You can write to Weber at the same time we can try to get it here.

Jaeger [board member]. *I make a motion to that effect. That one man be appointed.*

A. Will you do that Bob?

B. Yes.

A. There's a motion that we appoint a committee of one to make an investigation with regards the colored Local.

The minutes report the final outcome: "The secretary was instructed to write to Secretary Kernwood to ascertain the names and addresses of the officers of the recently organized colored musicians union. Motion was made and carried to appoint a delegate to investigate the colored local."

The issue of union versus non-union musicians, black versus white playing for black or white events and the idea that bands would play for less than scale was addressed again on November 12, 1926, during the weekly meeting of the board of directors of the Local No.174 AFM.

The minutes state, "O. Celestin, President of Local No. 496, in reply to an inquiry, declared that he did not know if the colored orchestra playing at the 'Jefferson Dance Hall' belonged to his local. And promised to turn the matter over to his business agent."

A week later, on November 19, 1926, the minutes from the meeting of the same board of directors state, "O. Celestin, president of Local # 496, colored, appeared with reference to our query as to whether it was a band from his Local who had played a certain engagement at the Jefferson Dance Hall. Celestin asserted that it was played by members of his Local, and as, in competitive engagements, they must receive no less a price than that fixed by this Local. Celestin was instructed with regard to it."

Chapter 13
Recording Sessions
1926–1928

On April 13, 1926, Celestin had a second recording session in New Orleans, this time with Columbia Records. The band at this session was Celestin (cnt), August Rousseau (tb), Earl Pierson (ts), Paul Barnes (as, cl), John Marrero (bj), Jeanette Salvant (p), Abby Foster (d, shouts) and Charles Gills (voc).

The four songs recorded that day were: "Station Calls," written by John Marrero; "I'm Satisfied You Love Me," written by John Marrero; "Give Me Some More," written by Barnes; and "My Josephine," co-written by Celestin and Barnes two years before. Each was recorded twice with the second take released. The song "My Josephine" had gone without a name until the band was playing at a function in Carrollton and a girl approached them, said she liked the tune and asked what it was called. The band asked her name, she replied, "Josephine," so they named it after her.

Bill Matthews identified the band for the first recording of "My Josephine" as Celestin (tp), Bill Matthews (tb), August Rousseau (tb), Paul Barnes (cl, sax), Sid Carriere (cl, ts), Simon Marrero (b) and John Marrero (bj).

Rousseau was the regular trombonist in the six- to eight-piece band, and Matthews was the regular trombonist in the fourteen-piece band. Matthews did not play the trombone on the recording that was used of "My Josephine." Alexis and Matthews agree that Alexis was the trumpet on the first recording of "My Josephine."

On April 11, 1927, the third recording session, again with Columbia Records, had Celestin leading a larger band. The players listed were Celestin and Ricard Alexis (tp), August Rousseau (tb), Paul Barnes (as), Earl Pierson (ts), Sid Carriere (sop, ts), John Marrero (bj), Simon Marrero (b, tu), Jeanette Salvant (p), Abby Foster (d, voc), Charles Gills (voc) and Ferdinand Joseph (voc).

The four songs recorded were "Dear Almanzoer," written by Celestin (one take); "As You Like It," written by Paul Barnes (one take); "Papa's Got the Jim Jams," written by John Marrero, with vocals by Foster (two takes, the second was released); and "Just For You Dear, I'm Crying," written by John Marrero with vocals by Ferdinand Joseph (three takes). Paul Barnes said, "'Just For You Dear, I'm Crying' was supposed to be the hit, instead it was 'My Josephine.' Shows how wrong musicians can be in predicting the public."

Ferdinand Joseph was the original name of vocalist Jelly Roll Morton. After checking the listing of households for the New Orleans area in 1926 and finding two other Ferdinand Josephs listed and then listening to an original copy of the recording, it is clear that this Ferdinand Joseph is not Jelly Roll Morton.

There were two other tunes recorded but never released, according to Foster: "Alamazon" and "A -Z Blues."

The fourth Columbia recording session was on October 25, 1927, with Celestin (tp), Ricard Alexis (tp) or George McCullum (tp), August Rousseau (tb) or Bill Mathews (tb), Clarence Hall (cl, as), Oliver Alcorn (cl, ts), Jeanette Salvant (p), John Marrero (bj), Simon Marrero (b) and Cie Frazier (d).

The two tunes recorded that day were "It's Jam Up," written by Celestin, arranged by Adolphe Alexander Sr. (two takes); and "When I'm With You," written by John Marrero (three takes).

On February 4, 1928, the *Chicago Defender* reported that the band personnel for a gig in Mobile, Alabama, was the same as for the October 25 recording session, except Foster replaced Frazier on drums and Joseph Lawrence was listed as the vocalist.

The final Columbia recording session in the 1920s was on December 13, 1928. The band was Celestin (tp), Guy Kelly (tp), Bill Mathews (tb), Ernest Kelly (tb), Earl Pierson (cl, as), Sid Carriere (cl, ts), Jeanette Salvant (p), Narvin Kimball (bj), Simon Marrero (b) and Abby Foster (d).

The two songs recorded were "The Sweetheart of T.K.O.," written by Julian James and Rupert Biggadike for the Theta Kappa Omega fraternity, (two takes), and "Ta-Ta Daddy," written by Celestin (two takes).

THE ORIGINAL TUXEDO JAZZ BAND

There were a total of six black New Orleans jazz bands recorded in the 1920s in New Orleans. The bands were Oscar "Papa" Celestin's Original Tuxedo Jazz Orchestra, Jones and Collins Astoria Hot Eight, Louis Dumaine's Jazzola Eight, Armand Piron's New Orleans Orchestra, Fate Marable's Society Syncopaters and Sam Morgan's Jazz Band.

Chapter 14
The Depression and War Years

As the Great Depression was starting in the late 1920s and early 1930s, the Tuxedo Band stayed busy touring the Gulf Coast states. The band played prestigious white dance jobs and carnival balls throughout the South and spot jobs or entire seasons at resorts like the Buena Vista and the White House Hotel in Biloxi. Celestin configured the band with anywhere from six to fourteen pieces and focused on keeping the dancers happy with a desirable swing dance beat. It was one of the more popular bands, known for its well-structured arrangements, tight musicianship and trumpet solos. Celestin, who was more restrained in his musical expression, encouraged the second trumpet to deliver the "hot" solos.

Josiah "Cie" Frazier talked with David Hillyer about his time with the band in Biloxi.

In 1930, I went over to Biloxi with [the] *Tuxedo Band to play that season job at the Buena Vista Hotel. I was playing with the Piron Band during them days and they* [Celestin] *asked me to play, that's a season job. It ends up in Labor Day. It's supposed to be ten weeks, something like that. Well, we used to play from 11:00 to 12:00 in the day, called breakfast dance. And then we played from 5:00 to 6:00, and then we come back and go play from 9:00 to 12:00, Mondays through Saturdays. And you had the Mississippi Blue Laws, we come home on Sunday, those who want to come home.*

Every Sunday, I had a four-cylinder Dodge car, well I used to drive home every Sunday and go back on Monday morning. Now I'll give you the members of that band. Yeah, first it had Bill Matthews on trombone, and

"Papa" Celestin on cornet and Ricard Alexis on cornet, two cornets, and the sax section consisted of a boy by the name of Son Johnson. He was good. Had Joe Rouzon, he's out of Los Angeles right now, on sax, another good man. And we had this boy Edmond, not Edmond Hall, this other one, Clarence Hall on tenor sax. Paul Barnes wasn't playing with the band at the time, not until the 1930s. Joe Rouzon got hurted, he kind of hurt his mouth, so they replaced him with this fellow here, Cecil Thornton. He's from St. Louis and he came down here on a boat. Not too much of a sax, but he was a terrible good arranger. They had him play with the band. He finished the thing. Then he started arranging for the band while we was on the season job. Mercedes [Fields] Gorman was playing the piano in Jeanette Salvant Kimball's place because she was expecting her first child.

Henry Kimball left the Desvigne Band to join the Tuxedo Band because he had fallen in love with Jeanette Salvant, the band's piano player. They were married June 4, 1929, and performed together with the band until 1935, when Jeanette took a long leave of absence to raise their children. She rejoined the band in 1953.

Narvin Kimball remembers the personnel of the band as Celestin (tp), Ricard Alexis (tp), Guy Kelly (tp), Bill Matthews (tb), Clarence Hall (as), Joe Rouzan (ts), Simon Marrero (b), Narvin Kimball (bj, g), Jeanette Salvant Kimball (p) and Cie Frazier (d). Spot players included Adolphe "Tats" Alexander Jr. (sax), Son Johnson (sax) and Cecil Thornton (sax).

Matthews remembered that the band played every year for five years straight in Biloxi at the White House and Buena Vista Hotel. Joe Rouson played sax with Celestin, as did Edmond Hall and Clarence Hall. Then Edmond Hall "jumped down," and they took Earl Pierson.

The *Louisiana Weekly* of October 25, 1930, reported the personnel of the band had changed a bit. "Celestin's Tuxedo 'Jazzers' included Celestin, first trumpeter and director; Richard Alexis, second trumpeter; W.M. Matthews, trombone; Cecil Thornton, first saxophonist; Augustus Johnson, third saxophonist; Clifford Jones, trap drummer; John Porter, sousaphonist; Henry Kimball Jr., banjoist and Mrs. Henry Kimball Jr., pianist."

In 1931, the band was again hired to play for the summer season at the Buena Vista Hotel in Biloxi. The band members that played that summer, not knowing it would be their last full-time job before they were affected by the Depression, were: Celestin (tp), Henry "Kildee" Holloway (tp), Ricard Alexis (tp), Bill Mathews (tb), Adolphe Alexander Jr. (sax), Son Johnson (sax), Cecil Thornton (sax), Narvin Kimball (b) and Cie Frazier (d).

Frazier had replaced Foster as the regular drummer and played with Celestin for a while in the 1930s before he returned the drums to Foster and told him he couldn't hold the job. When Foster asked why, Frazier explained that the band played twenty-two choruses of "High Society" and then told him to go out "hot." The band told him Foster could do it, but Frazier said he himself could not. Frazier asked Foster to take back the job, but Foster refused. Celestin hired "Black Happy" Goldston to take over as the regular drummer, and he stayed with the band through the early 1950s until Louis Barbarin became the drummer.

Goldston fondly remembered touring around the South, though along with the sweet times, there were the occasional hardships. He remembered Celestin buying a big, second-hand car to take the six-piece band on the road. The band was booked all over the Gulf Coast, and the car made the travel easier than if they were using a bus or train. They played their jobs, driving from gig to gig and making good money. The car broke down, and they had to spend most of that money to get the car fixed so they could get home.

The cutting contests continued, as an advertisement in the November 28, 1931 issue of the *Louisiana Weekly* proclaimed. "Don't forget Professor Celestin's Tuxedo Orchestra vs. Anthony St. Leger's Orchestra. Sunday Nov. 29, 1931, 26 Pelican Garden, From 6 o'clock till late. Admission, 30 cents."

In 1932, with the Depression forcing many people to cut back on everything, Celestin left his full-time job as a musician and was easily rehired as a longshoreman in New Orleans. He and the other band members continued to play weekends and private jobs in New Orleans, but they stopped their rigorous touring. As Bill Matthews said, "The Depression came along. The Tuxedo Band played in and out, gig work, played every place you could play. Then the boys got to splitting up, Guy [Kelly] went away, Paul Barnes went away. Things were really dead. This made a big change with the band."

Homer Dupuy, an uptown gentleman, had his opinion of what happened to the band during the Depression.

I think one thing of interest is that during the war, Papa Celestin, who rose to great heights locally, here in New Orleans, to give you some idea as to how people felt about jazz, or at least maybe there just wasn't enough manpower to do it during the war. Papa Celestin gave up the leadership of his band, I think it dissolved and he was a chauffeur. It wasn't until after the war that the revision of the enthusiasm for jazz, that his band collected again. And he became one of the outstanding people in this part of the country on jazz.

Celestin's band was consistently chosen for any prestigious job, especially when the managers of the event wanted to ensure a huge turnout. This advertisement ran in the *Louisiana Weekly* on September 3, 1932: "Papa Celestin and the Tuxedo Jazz Band will re-open the doors of the renovated Astoria Night Club, Sunday and Monday night. They are expecting the largest dance crowd in the history of the hall."

Three weeks later, in the September 24, 1932 issue of the *Louisiana Weekly* came this upsetting news with its curious headline.

Police Corporal Aids in Attack on Celestin

Oscar "Papa" Celestin left a gig at Astoria Gardens at 3 in the morning after Labor Day and walked to the corner of Canal and Royal to await the arrival of his car [streetcar], the same one he would catch after all his late nights. No car was there so he walked to the Woolworth's window to look at post cards.

A man came along and knocked me off the banquette [sidewalk], saying "Get the hell out of the way."

The man continued on his way then a car pulled up and they talked. The man that had first attacked me began walking in my direction yet he appeared not to be noticing me. Just as he was passing behind me, he drew a crank from behind him and hit me in the face. I immediately grabbed him, throwing him to the ground and started calling for help. A crowd gathered as the police came up.

The police took the crank from the man, told me to stand against the wall. I did and then saw my hat on the ground. An officer searched me, found $35 and I told the police it was for the work I had just done. I asked the police to be allowed to pick up my hat. The police said I could, I did and then I returned to stand by the wall. While standing there by the wall I said, "I have been living here for twenty five years but have never been in any kind of trouble, and then this had to happen."

The corporal then struck me a heavy blow in the back of the neck which almost broke my bones. I said no more and was taken to the Third precinct where the officers wanted to place me in jail, without going to the hospital.

One of the officers knew him and he was taken to the hospital to have his wounds dressed.

From the time of my arrival at the third precinct, the officers refused to allow me a chance to call any one and tell of my arrest. At the hospital I attempted to telephone again and was refused, yet when I was returned to the third precinct, the officers allowed me to call my wife.

After that I selected my cell and remained there until I was able to secure my bond.

He had offered no resistance and is now recovering at his residence on France Street.

The March 18, 1933 issue of the *Louisiana Weekly* reported that Celestin and the Tuxedo Band were on the road, and it being the middle of March, they were using "If You Can't Dance You'll Shiver" as their theme song. "Orchestras may go and orchestras may come, but Celestin's will live on forever in your memory if you ever listen to their haunting melodies that just tantalize your very being and make you forget your troubles. Celestin has succeeded in securing the services of some of the best young musicians in the South and has real discipline."

Celestin (tp) was traveling with Herman Franklin (tp), Henry Holloway (tp, arr), William N. Matthews (tb), Myer Kennedy (cl, sax), Clarence Hall

Tuxedo Jazz Orchestra, 1931. *Left to right:* Bill Matthews, Henry Holloway, Oscar Celestin, Herman Franklin, Meyer Kennedy, Joe Laurence, Clarence Hall, Oliver Alcorn, Louis Barbarin, John Porter, Jeanette Kimball and Narvin Kimball. *Courtesy of the Hogan Jazz Archive, Tulane University.*

(ts, as), Narvin Kimball Jr (bj, arr), John Porter (sousa), Jeanette Salvant Kimball (p), Lucien Barbarin (d) and Joseph Addison Lawrence (ent).

Forgetting your troubles was a good reason to go see a band in the middle of the Depression, if you could afford the cover of between ten and fifty cents.

In the early 1940s, swing tunes like "In the Mood" and "Don't Get Around Much Anymore" were popular, and Celestin and the band were playing them along with their standards. A configuration of the band from 1940 included Celestin (tp), Herman Franklin (tp), Wendell Eugene (tb), Raz "Butch" Roseby (tb), Robert Hall (ts), John Patterson (ts), "Squeak" Joseph (as), Joe Harris (as), John Porter (b), Adam Cato (p) and Dave Robert "Bob" Ogden (d). On occasion, Wendell Eugene requested the addition of Henry Ross (tp), Louis "Big Eye" Nelson (tb), Tom Johnson (as) and Narvin Kimball (b).

The West End was a tourist destination on the shore of Lake Pontchartrain, at the end of the West End Boulevard. There was streetcar service to the popular place where New Orleanians could spend time enjoying the nightlife. The Southern Yacht Club was located there, as were restaurants and nightclubs. In late 1939 or early 1940, the West End Tavern opened, and trombonist Hamp Benson (tb) put together a band with Celestin (tp), Bill Matthews (tb), Alphonse Picou (cl) and Steve Lewis (p). They played together at that gig for only six to eight months, when Camp Leroy Johnson was created and the lakefront was taken over by the United States military and closed to civilians for the duration of World War II.

During World War II, Celestin continued to lead the Tuxedo Jazz Orchestra while he worked in a shipyard as a welder. In the early 1940s, to cater to the local interest for more danceable swing-style music, he added some new players to the band: Captain John Handy (as), Jimmy "Kid" Clayton (tp), Wallace Davenport (tp) and Octave Crosby (p).

In 1944, Celestin was struck and run over by a truck while at the shipyard. He spent almost a year in the hospital with two severely broken legs and then quite a while recuperating at home. The breaks in his legs never healed correctly, and from then on he walked with a slight limp.

John G. Curran, talking about the New Orleans Jazz comeback, said:

> *Well, it was not that so much as a question of lack of interest. The Dixieland bands, the white bands, they all left New Orleans and to put it bluntly, the Dixieland bands that remained in New Orleans at the time of*

Oscar Celestin, recuperating from a broken leg in 1945. *Courtesy of the Hogan Jazz Archive, Tulane University.*

Pearl Harbor, well, they just broke up more than anything. Papa Celestin called his band together the night of Pearl Harbor and said, "We've played our last note of music." It was war, and that was the end of it. But it came back, after the war, and it came back in quite a rush. When it came back it was not limited to New Orleans. It was through the entire U.S., and the entire world.

Chapter 15
Comeback
1940–1950s

"Black Happy" Goldston, who as a child had beat out rhythms on steps using chair rungs as drumsticks, and Bill Matthews, who worked the shipyards with Celestin, were the two musicians that stuck with Celestin through the Depression and the time Celestin spent healing from his broken legs. Toward the end of World War II, with traditional jazz being revived and both the New Orleans Jazz Club and his wife, Sarah, urging him to make a comeback, Celestin and the band started rehearsing two to three times a week and soon announced that "Papa" Celestin's Tuxedo Jazz Band—with Celestin (tp), Bill Matthews (tb), Alphonse Picou (cl), Ricard Alexis (b), Mercedes "Candy" Fields (p) and "Black Happy" Goldston (d)—would be making a comeback. As Elizabeth O'Kelly Kerrigan said, "I think Celestin got his start back here at the Pass [Pass Christian] because you know, John Curran got him to come over here, because all of our generation just loved it, and the kids picked it up and then they started playing it in New Orleans again."

During the 1946–47 tourist season, Celestin auditioned to work for the National Jazz Foundation. John G. Curran said, "In the early to mid-'30s, they just didn't have any Dixieland bands at all during that time. Then the New Orleans Jazz Foundation got busy, and they started out, the first band they started out with was Bunk Johnson's band, they brought him back."

The band was hired, and the comeback of the Tuxedo Jazz Orchestra was underway. The band's first night back was described in the article "Papa's Horn Of Plenty," by James Leslie, who wrote, "The crowd began gathering in a Bourbon Street nightclub. By 9:30 the place was jammed to capacity and the crowd had overflowed into the street. Emerging from the smoky room was the scream of 'Papa's' horn, almost exactly as it sounded at Tom Anderson's saloon 50 years earlier."

Celestin said in an interview for the July 6, 1953 issue of the *New Orleans Times-Picayune*, "When I get warm and my lips are right, the music comes pouring out." And when asked what he has learned to play over the years that his audiences like the most, he had a one-word answer: "Loud."

The musicians joining him in this much-welcomed comeback were: "Kid Shots" Madison (tr), Bill Mathews (tb), Alphonse Picou and Willie Humphrey (cl), Albert French (bj), Leonard Mitchell (g), Ricard Alexis (b), Jeanette Salvant Kimball (p) and "Black Happy" Goldston (d).

On October 26, 1947, the band was back in the studio recording, this time for Deluxe Records as Celestin's Original Tuxedo Orchestra. The players listed were Celestin (tp), Bill Mathews (tb), Alphonse Picou (cl), Paul Barnes (as), Sam Lee (ts), Harrison Veret (g), Ricard Alexis (b), Mercedes Fields (p) and "Black Happy" Goldston (d).

The band recorded "Eh La Bas," "Marie Laveau," "My Josephine" and "Maryland, My Maryland." A short time after the session, Celestin told a reporter that he was working on three new tunes: "Atomic Control," "Papa Celestin's Hop" and "Trying To Get Along." None of these was ever recorded.

"Black Happy" Goldston recalled:

When they made records, they had to be quiet; it was a hot process, cutting them over and over. They didn't want you to imitate anyone; you had to play your own style.

They'd get a keg of beer for $1.25, sometimes they'd buy ham, bread, potato salad, hot dogs and after rehearsal they'd eat and drink. Sometimes they'd have a big plate of red beans and rice, ham gumbo and chicken. The little boys could drink inside someone's home then.

Bourbon Street in the late 1940s and early 1950s was the epicenter of the New Orleans Jazz Revival, with nightclubs filling the blocks between Canal Street and St Louis Street. Jazz was played all over the city, but Bourbon Street had the greatest concentration of Jazz Clubs per block. One of the more popular clubs was the Paddock Lounge, at 315 Bourbon Street, owned by Steve Valenti and decorated with a horse-racing theme. The bandstand, directly behind the horseshoe-shaped bar, was chest high with just enough headroom for the taller men to be able to keep from hitting the ceiling. A small barrier separated the musicians' feet from the bartender's bottle selection. Patrons seated at the bar could watch the performance happening less than five feet from their drinks. Or they could look at small horse models, a concrete jockey and silver trophies gathered from long-ago horse races scattered around the edge of the platform.

Lester Alexis, the younger brother of Celestin's bass player, Ricard Alexis, was playing drums in a combo at the Paddock Lounge when he was approached by Mr. Valenti, who wanted to try a Dixieland band in the club. He asked Lester to bring his brother Ricard by so he could talk to him. Valenti asked Ricard to put together a band but stipulated that he wanted a man, not a woman, to play the piano. Alexis agreed, they worked out the financial compensation and then Valenti told him the band was to start Saturday, two nights away.

Alexis called Bill Matthews at midnight and told him, "You've got a job, man, on Bourbon Street."

Alexis and Matthews were both regulars in Celestin's band, so they decided to raid the rest of the musicians for this new Saturday night gig. Alexis said he'd get Octave Crosby for the piano. When they added Goldston on drums, Celestin heard about the new gig and told Alexis, "Get who you want, but I'm not going to lead my band out here. I'm not going to play here to help you build it up, because I got too much work coming up." Matthews and Goldston assured Celestin they would not be leaving the Tuxedo, just keeping a steady job with Alexis on Saturday nights.

Then Alexis hired Celestin.

The first six months of the Saturday night gig at the Paddock, Celestin worked for Alexis's band until Alexis gave up the leadership and Celestin took the job for the next six months.

As Bill Matthews remembers, "Everything was Papa Celestin. Papa was very sick then, but he worked there a few years, got himself straightened out, stopped fooling around. He didn't want to work anymore; he didn't know how to quit. Finally he jumped down."

Celestin had approached William Houston, the president of AFM Local 496, a man who Celestin thought was "all tied up with Mr. Steve Valenti" and could influence Valenti in matters concerning Celestin's employment at the Paddock. Celestin told Houston he wanted to get his own band in there, his band that he had on the outside, not the one he had taken over from Ricard Alexis. At the time, he was being paid $75.00 a week, but he told Houston he wanted that upped to $300.00.

Matthews got wind of that conversation and told Celestin that he must not want to work there. Celestin replied to him, "You're right Billy, you're

Celestin's Band at the Paddock, 1953–54. *Left to right:* Octave Crosby, Black Happy Goldston, Ricard Alexis, Oscar Celestin, Alphonse Picou and Bill Matthews. *Courtesy of the Hogan Jazz Archive, Tulane University.*

right. I don't want to work there. If you give me $300 a week I'll work and I'll work with my other band."

Celestin asked Matthews what he intended to do, and Matthews said he intended to stick on the job he had with Alexis. "Ricard Alexis brought us here, and I'm working. I'm making a great improvement in it. You'll get on out there and make another band up yourself. That's all you can do. It'll be okay with me. Any time I happen to need you, I'll ask you for a job. That's all I can do."

Celestin had kept his regular Tuxedo Jazz Band for his steady gigs while he was also working at the Paddock with the Alexis band. He continued to lead that band after leaving the Paddock. When Matthews was interviewed by Bill Russell in 1959, he was still with the Alexis band, working at the Paddock.

Celestin told a reporter from the *Times-Picayune* that his "biggest thrill came in 1949":

Believe it or not, I've played for three generations of some families like the Westfeldts, Jahnckes and McLaughlins. The old folks got together and hired me to play at the Valencia Club at 1900 Valence St. My audience was entirely 9 and 10 year old children. Best time I ever had in my life was signing autographs for those youngsters who'd come up and say, "My grandmother hired you to play at the old Southern Yacht Club," or "My grandfather says he used to dance to your music 30 years ago." Shucks, I signed autographs for half an hour; I've never had such a good time.

John G. Curran explained to David Hillyer about the popularity of Celestin and his band.

Celestin has said that he has played for debutantes and he has played for those debutantes' grandmothers at their debut party, because he did play in New Orleans over a period of 50 years. And he was accepted as a real heritage in New Orleans of all the colored musicians, because he was the one, single leader who refused to leave New Orleans for more than thirty days. He never left New Orleans, regardless of how much money was

Celestin and his band in a restaurant. *Left to right:* Black Happy Goldston, Octave Crosby, Ricard Alexis, Alphonse Picou and Bill Matthews.

offered him to leave. There are certain families in New Orleans who have been here for generation and generations that just could not have a debut party without Celestin or Celestin's band playing for that particular party.

Abagail Arnold agreed with Curran and told Hillyer:

Well, they'd usually have Celestin for serious dances, like sorority dances. It was just sort of the style that, when you were going to have a serious dance, you had to have semi-serious music. I think Celestin's band can be considered one of the best jazz bands in the country. But not as a program that you would sit and listen to. I think you can hear the best jazz at a party because I think that part of jazz is its reaction in its audience, and that comes best at a party rather than a concert atmosphere.

Leigh Carrole III voiced her opinion to Hillyer, saying, "I heard 'Papa' Celestin's band when I was about twelve (in 1950) at the old yacht club. For dances from 1950 to 1953, the majority of social functions, certainly, everybody was trying to get Celestin. He was in great demand. If they didn't have Celestin, they just had a pops band, which nobody could stand."

Chapter 16

On the Docks and at the White House

In late 1949, Celestin and his Tuxedo Jazz Band were recorded live during WDSU radio's Saturday night broadcasts of *Roger Wolfe's New Orleans Bandwagon*. Throughout 1950, DJ Roger Wolfe continued live broadcasting of *The Dixieland Jambake*. The show followed the format of ABC's *Battle of the Bands*, with competing bands having airtime to showcase their individual styles.

Sharkey Bonanno and his band or Frank Assunto with the Dukes of Dixieland were usually pitted against Celestin and his Tuxedo Jazz Band. Celestin (tp) led his regular band of Bill Matthews (tb), Alphonse Picou (cl), Ricard Alexis (b, voc), Octave Crosby (p) and "Black Happy" Goldston (d).

The tunes recorded were pulled from their popular set list and are listed in the discography at the end of this book.

A number of LPs were released by New Orleans Bandwagon, Jazzology, Racoon, Fairmont and Southland Records with various combinations of the tunes from these shows. Bootleg albums have also been released to the public featuring these recordings.

In a 1962 interview for the Hogan Jazz Archives, Goldston said, "In 1961, WDSU called all the musicians on that record down and gave them checks for sixty-five dollars."

An article in the *Old French Quarter News* in 1950 reported that the Tuxedo Band was playing Sunday afternoons on WTPS between 3:00 and 3:30 during the Regal Beer show.

Celestin and the band maintained their regular club dates at the Paddock Lounge on Bourbon Street, with spot jobs at the Mardi Gras Lounge and the Famous Door. They continued to be in constant demand for private

More than a Century of a New Orleans Icon

Celestin's Tuxedo Jazz Band (tan suits), Frank Assunto's Original Dukes of Dixieland (striped jackets), Paul Barbarin's Jazz Band (white jackets) and Pete Fountain's Band (dark suits) playing at the New Orleans Municipal Auditorium in 1953. *Courtesy of the Estate of Frank J. Assunto.*

parties and college dances, and during carnival season, which runs from January 6 through Mardi Gras Day, they had a steady stream of social clubs and krewes that wouldn't be happy with any other band.

As Marietta M. Moyer recalls:

> *When I was a teen and I started going to parties and dances, they always had, or usually had, a jazz band. When they didn't have a jazz band, say at a formal, and they just had a regular dance band, they always played the New Orleans jazz because it was expected. The most popular of course, was Papa Celestin. I think anytime there was a party where there was a jazz band, they would always call him first. There was George Lewis and several others, I remember* [Frank Assunto and] *the Dukes of Dixieland, which is a white band. Even though they were very good they still didn't have the rhythm or the spirit that the Negro band at the Paddock had.*

Celestin and the band continued to travel and perform throughout the Gulf South. On Thursday, October 26, 1950, the Cultural Entertainment Committee of the University of Texas presented Oscar "Papa" Celestin and his Tuxedo Dixieland Jazz Band in concert in the Gregory Gymnasium at 8:15 pm. This was one in a series of classical performances that included traveling orchestras, operas and ballet.

The set list from that program included: "Basin Street Blues"; "South Rampart Street Parade"; "Way Down Yonder in New Orleans"; "High Society"; "When the Saints Go Marching In"; "Siboney," featuring Pork Chops the Entertainer; "Marie Laveau"; "Peanut Vendor"; "Won't You Come Home Bill Bailey"; "Who Threw the Whiskey in the Well"; "Ole' Man Mose"; "Oh Didn't He Ramble"; "Maryland, My Maryland"; and "I'll Be Glad When You're Dead, You Rascal You" before the intermission.

They resumed the evening's concert with: "Clarinet Marmalade"; "Milneburg Joys"; "Just a Closer Walk With Thee"; "Whenever You're Lonesome Just Telephone Me"; "Careless Love"; "Tiger Rag"; "Fidgety Feet," featuring Pork Chops the Entertainer; "St. Louis Blues"; "Mona Lisa"; "Twelfth Street Rag"; "Pine Top Boogie"; "Lil' Liza Jane"; and "Good Night Irene," one of Celestin's favorite songs to close out an evening.

The band that evening was listed as: Celestin (tr), Eddie Pierson (tb), Paul Barnes (cl), Harrison Verret (g), John Porter (b), Lionel Reason (p), Louis Barbarin (d) and Pork Chops, tap dancer.

The band was in the recording studio from late 1950 to late 1951 in New Orleans with many of the individual tunes being released on vinyl under different labels.

Celestin's Band on WDSU radio, circa 1950. *Left to right:* Harrison Verret, John Porter, Eddie Pierson, Louis Barbarin, Adolphe Alexander, Oscar Celestin and Mercedes Fields. *Courtesy of the New Orleans Jazz Club Collection of the Louisiana State Museum.*

The Mississippi Shipping Company hired Celestin's band to serenade its cruise passengers while they traversed the dock. The men in the band were required to wear clothing more often seen on a farm than in town. The tourism industry wanted to create the image of uneducated happy-go-lucky musicians who would be grateful for a few tossed coins. The musicians chose to tolerate playing the role because the shipping company paid well.

Between the nightly jobs on Bourbon Street, where they continued to wear their usual suits or tuxedos, and the job on the docks with its more relaxed dress code, Celestin and his band became one of the city's most popular tourist attractions. They also maintained a loyal, multi-generational following of locals. Papa was often heard to say, "Honey chile, I not only knows you, but I knows yo' daddy and yo' granddaddy."

When David Hillyer asked William Renaudin if jazz was popular, he replied, "Parties I attended usually had a Dixieland jazz band to supply the music. The fraternity I was in would hire colored jazz bands; white jazz bands weren't as popular. These bands seemed to be respected; in fact the type of music was respected a great deal, by the people that were at the parties." Esther Dupuy agreed and added, "All the parties I ever went to in New Orleans we danced to jazz music. Except during the war and when I was away most of the time and sometimes I went from the newspaper to cover, for pictures and things, and sometimes friends of mine, their daughters would make their debut and I would go, and it seems to me the most popular form of music all through these years has been our Dixieland colored bands." John G. Curran summed it up by saying, "It's standard in New Orleans, whether at parties in the afternoon or at night, or at breakfast parties in the morning. It's just something that goes with New Orleans."

Mel Leavitt, of the *New Orleans Clarion Herald*, reported that he overheard a guest at a sugar bowl party say to Papa Celestin, "You must like it here in New Orleans, Papa...you must like it very much."

"Man," Papa said, smiling all over, "if I likes New Orleans any mo'...I eats New Orleans up."

In early 1951, Celestin traveled to California with plans to spend a few months enjoying a much-needed rest hoping to regain his health. He left Mathews, his trombone player, in charge of fronting the band at its regular gig at the Paddock. While Celestin was in California, he looked up his old friend and trombone player, Edward "Kid" Ory. Celestin booked a four-week job playing together with Ory and his band at the Beverly Caverns. The tension created by having two men trying to lead one band sent Celestin back to New Orleans sooner than he had planned.

Upon his return, he found that Mathews had quit the Paddock Lounge, put his own band together with a number of musicians from Celestin's band and was playing a regular gig at the Mardi Gras Lounge.

Celestin put together a new group of musicians and was soon back playing at the Paddock Lounge. The newest formation of the band featured Celestin on trumpet with Eddie Pierson (tb), Joseph Thomas (cl), Adolphe Alexander Jr. (as), Albert French (bj), Sidney Brown (b), Jeanette Kimball (p) and Cie Frazier or Louis Barbarin (d).

On May 8, 1953, Celestin and the Original Tuxedo Jazz Band had the honor of being the first New Orleans jazz band to play at the White House in a special performance for President Eisenhower at the Annual Banquet of the White House Correspondents' Association.

In a May 6, 1953 article in *the New Orleans Times-Picayune*, Celestin was asked about the upcoming trip to Washington, D.C.

"Were they nervous?" Reporter Walter Goldstein asked Celestin about the band.

"No, man," said Celestin, "Thrilled and excited? Yes, but not nervous. Why, we're just going there and be ourselves and give them the same kind of music as we give the wonderful people of New Orleans.

"The whole band will make the trip," he said. "Edward Pierson on trombone, Adolphe Alexander on the saxophone and clarinet. Louis Barbarin on drums, Albert French on guitar and banjo, Sidney Brown on bass, Jeanette Salvant on piano and yours truly."

Celestin said they would start with "Basin Street Blues" then on to "High Society," "When the Saints Go Marching In," "Darktown Strutters Ball," "Way Down Yonder in New Orleans," "Maryland, My Maryland," "Tailgate Ramble" and "Didn't He Ramble."

Celestin said the boys hoped for warm weather in Washington so that they could deck out in white dinner jackets and maroon bow ties for their stint at the dinner.

"Of course, I'll be wearing that blood-red tie," he said, "and my gold trumpet in my lapel, and that tie clasp with the notes of the scale on it."

The band will be working gratis, with permission from James C. Petrillo, president of the American Association of Musicians. The White House Correspondents Association is paying their expenses.

At that event, when he received the White House Press Correspondents Association's Certificate of Honor, Celestin said, "I feel that I have made a wonderful mark and a wonderful success as a native-born Southerner to have the opportunity to play at this dinner."

President Eisenhower shook Celestin's hand at the end of the performance and said, "Mr. Celestin, you are a fine gentleman and a credit to your race and our country." Celestin declared it "the proudest moment of my life." There was a recording made to commemorate the event, limited to a pressing of one hundred copies. Louisiana congressman F. Edward Hebert gave Papa a recording of the entire proceedings.

Chapter 17

Celestin's Last Years

S tart-up festivals and yearly events are a much-loved component of the culture of Louisiana in general and New Orleans in particular. Celestin and the band were hired to play the first annual New Orleans Creole Festival, an open-air concert for La Creole Fete Association de Nouvelle Orleans (the New Orleans Creole Fiesta Association), a group founded in 1952 by Mrs. A.C. Synigal, who also served as its president. The festival was held in Beauregard Square on Monday, July 27, 1953, at 8:00 p.m.

In 1948, the New Orleans Jazz Club was founded by Albert Diket, Johnny (Hyman) Wiggs, Gilbert Erskine and Donald Perry, and in 1949, the club sponsored its first festival. It was held in Congo Square and was the forerunner to the Jazz and Heritage Festival still held in New Orleans in the spring of every year.

Celestin and the band were hired to play the festival in August 1949. The members of the band for that first fest were Celestin (tp), Bill Matthews (tb), Alphonse Picou (cl), Harrison Verret (g,bj), Ricard Alexis (b), Octave Crosby (p) and "Black Happy" Goldston (d). In 1953, they were back on stage at the New Orleans Municipal Auditorium performing for the fifth year in a row.

Opposite, top: Creole Fiesta Association, circa 1950. *Left to right:* Madame A.C. Synigal, Mrs. Vera Falgout, Beulah Frank Jones (Mrs. Louis) Augustine, Mrs. Vivian Yates and Miss Geraldine B. Talton. *Courtesy of the Hogan Jazz Archive, Tulane University.*

Opposite, bottom: Celestin's band on stage in Congo Square for an early Jazz Fest, circa 1950. *Left to right:* Octave Crosby, Ricard Alexis, Harrison Verret, Black Happy Goldston, Oscar Celestin, Alphonse Picou and Bill Matthews. *Courtesy of the Hogan Jazz Archive, Tulane University.*

In November 1953, Celestin and his Tuxedo Dixieland Band were in Cosimo Matassa's studio recording "Tiger Rag" and "At the Darktown Strutters Ball," with a spoken introduction by Celestin. Both tunes were recorded for the soundtrack of the movie *Cinematic Holiday*, in which Celestin and the band performed. The filming took place at the Absinthe House, where the band was playing a regular job at the time, and was done with three synchronized projectors to create a panoramic effect. Celestin, in his late sixties, was captured on film looking vibrant while performing his spirited versions of many New Orleans standards. In fact, his health was failing, and he was spending extended periods of time resting.

Only "Tiger Rag" was used in the soundtrack, but Columbia Records issued a two-sided vinyl album with both songs in conjunction with the release of the movie, which resulted in a large financial bonus for Celestin. Author James Leslie remembers the standard Celestin routine on "Tiger Rag." "He would claw the air like a caged tiger; roar into the microphone; look askance from side to side; then roll his eyes and go through the clowning act all over again."

The band that preformed in the movie consisted of Celestin and Ricard Alexis (tp), Eddie Pierson (tb), Joseph Thomas (cl), Emanuel Paul (ts), Adolphe Alexander Jr. (as), Albert French (bj), Sidney Brown (b), Jeanette Kimball (p) and Louis Barbarin (d).

In late April 1954, Celestin recorded at the Southland Studios for the last time. Joe Mares was in charge of the session, at which five songs were recorded. The band members in the studio joining Celestin were Eddie Pierson (tb), Adolphe Alexander Jr (as), Joseph Thomas (cl), Albert French (bj,g), Jeanette Kimball (p), Sidney Brown (b) and Louis Barbarin (d).

The four songs that made it to the ten-inch vinyl LP were "Marie LaVeau," "Down By the Riverside," "When the Saints Go Marching In" and "Oh Didn't He Ramble." Also recorded but not released was "Do You Know What it Means to Miss New Orleans."

The record, entitled *Papa's Golden Wedding*, was released to commemorate his fifty years as a trumpeter. Celestin was quite ill at the time, but no one realized it would be the final time he played the trumpet in public.

Ridgley, who had stopped playing music back in 1931 when he joined the church, felt he had prolonged his own life by giving up music and the lifestyle that went with it. He encouraged others to do the same and tried to get Celestin to quit many times as he got older, but Celestin wouldn't because he loved it too much. Ridgley said that when he visited Celestin in the hospital the last time, Celestin said to him, "Ridgley, if I ever get over this, I'll never pick up that horn again."

Celestin's Band, circa 1954. *Left to right:* John Porter, Jeanette Kimball, Albert French, "Cornbread" Thomas, Alvin Alcorn, Sarah Celestin, Oscar Celestin, Louis Barbarin and Eddie Pierson. *Courtesy of the French Family Archive.*

Oscar Phillip "Papa" Celestin died from cancer at the age of seventy on Wednesday, December 15, 1954, at his home on 2326 France Street in New Orleans. Survivors listed in the *Times-Picayune* obituary included his wife of thirty-two years, Sarah Jackson Celestin, originally of Morgan City, and Mrs. Hannah Parker, his niece from California.

The December 16 *States-Item* reported that at 9:00 p.m. that Wednesday, the first three visitors had signed the "Shrine of Memories" booklet where friends and family of the deceased may register. The first to sign was Mayor DeLesseps S. "Chep" Morrison. The second was patrolman Edward Hirstius, the mayor's chauffer, and the third was the president of the chamber of commerce, George S. Dinwiddie.

The viewing was held Friday, December 17, at the Gertrude Geddes Willis funeral home at 2120 Jackson Avenue, with thousands standing in line before the doors opened at 4:30 p.m. Willis J. Misshore, the funeral director, said, "They've [the masses of people] been calling for twenty-

Celestin's casket at Geddes Funeral Parlour, 1954. Band members are in the second row, and family is in the first. *Courtesy of the New Orleans Jazz Club Collection of the Louisiana State Museum.*

eight hours." Though there were still people waiting to view the body of the much-loved musician, the doors to the funeral home had to be closed at midnight for the private Masonic service for Celestin, a thirty-second-degree Mason with the Prince Hall affiliation of Richmond Lodge No. 1, F&AM; Eureka Consistory No. 7, ASRFM and Radiant Chapter No. 1, RAM.

On Saturday morning, the Eureka Brass Band "played the body out" of the funeral home with a version of "Just A Little While to Stay Here." The pallbearers—Edward Pierson, Joseph "Brother Cornbread" Thomas, Sidney Brown, Louis Barbarin, Adolphe Alexander and Albert French, all six members of Celestin's Tuxedo Jazz Band—put his casket into the hearse for the ride to the Mount Zion Methodist Church, located at 2722 Louisiana Avenue. Jeanette Kimball, the band's pianist, rode in the car with the musician's family.

Esther Dupuy Breckenridge, a reporter who attended the funeral, said, "Celestin was a hero to me. I went to the funeral and being a member of the press, we were very near his coffin. It was a beautiful ceremony, very interesting, highly religious but, I think, a great, great loss to New Orleans."

More than a Century of a New Orleans Icon

Celestin's funeral procession, 1954. *Courtesy of the New Orleans Jazz Club Collection of the Louisiana State Museum.*

After the service, it took the pallbearers thirty minutes to carry the casket from the church through the crowd to the hearse. Everyone wanted to touch the silver-trimmed, gray casket. Police reinforcements were called in from as far away as Canal Street to help keep order of the estimated ten thousand people that lined the streets, waiting to pay their last respects.

The Eureka Brass Band and members of the Original Tuxedo Brass Band were playing "Just a Closer Walk With Thee," a final request of Papa's, as the fifteen black limousines filled with family members and close friends started the first part of the trek to the cemetery. An estimated four thousand admirers and friends following on foot made up the second line for the thirteen-block walk up Louisiana Avenue to Broad Avenue. The bands were playing "What A Friend We Have In Jesus" when they reached Broad Avenue. There they boarded buses for the final leg of the trip to Mount Olivet Cemetery at 4000 Norman Mayer, in the Gentilly area near Dillard University.

It was after 5:00 p.m. and almost dark when the band "played him home" at the grave (Unit 1, section B, no. 447) with "Just A Closer Walk With Thee." The graveside service was conducted by Reverend Hill and members of the Masonic Lodge French Hall, Eureka Consistory No. 1.

As Keith C. Marshall reported in the *Times-Picayune* in November 1999, "When the casket containing the beloved Negro musician was lowered into a tomb in Mount Olivet cemetery…the two bands at graveside broke up and left the cemetery, thus ending a four hour funeral. They left a graveyard crowd of one thousand stunned, for many had expected to hear the bands cut loose with the songs of rejoicing that traditionally end a jazz funeral."

Another article from the *Times-Picayune* quoted one of the musicians as saying, "We thought out of respect for Papa it would be better not to play

Celestin's funeral at the cemetery with Eureka Brass Band, 1954. *Courtesy of the Hogan Jazz Archive, Tulane University.*

any jazz." Another musician felt it was too late and dark in the unlit cemetery to be playing any more.

New Orleans States columnist Pie Dufour mused on Celestin's homecoming. "Gabriel knows a horn blower when he hears one and I don't doubt but that he's been saying to 'Papa' for several days now. 'C'mon, Papa, play "When the Saints Go Marchin' In" again.'"

Celestin, especially since his comeback in the late 1940s, had become a truly beloved institution in New Orleans. As Klaus Berenbrok wrote in *Melody-Maker* in January 1955, "Papa Celestin must be regarded as one of the pioneers of jazz cornet playing, along with Joe Oliver, Freddy Keppard and Mutt Carey. His first recordings were with the Original Tuxedo Jazz Orchestra for Okeh in 1925, and are really splendid examples of New

Orleans jazz at its best, well recorded and well played. With brilliant cornet duets by Celestin and Kid Shots Madison."

He was a competent trumpeter and an outstanding leader who was able to configure remarkable bands. As William Bebe Ridgley said in an interview with Richard B. Allen and David Dutcher in April 1961, "Some people liked Mutt Carey, 'Shots' Madison or Buddy Petit's style of playing better, but Celestin had the ability to get along with people. Celestin was such a nice guy, everybody liked him."

In early 1954, the Jazz Foundation of New Orleans (the New Orleans Jazz Club) wanted to honor the man who had given so much to his audiences locally and worldwide. The foundation commissioned sculptor Rai Granier Murray to create a bust of "Papa" Celestin and placed the sculpture in the Delgado Museum (currently known as the New Orleans Museum of Art). It was to have been dedicated on December 15, the day Celestin died.

Janeth McKendrick, daughter of sculptor Rai Murray, mentioned in a *Times-Picayune* article in May 1991 that she and her mother would go to the Paddock to listen to Papa Celestin's Tuxedo Jazz Band frequently. She remembers the tunes "Little Liza Jane" and "Marie Laveau" as favorites that were played all the time.

The January 9, 1955 edition of the *New Orleans Times-Picayune* reported, "Sculptured Celestin Head Given to Library" and included a description of the ceremony.

New Orleans librarian John Hall Jacobs was the Master of Ceremonies. Celestin's niece, Mrs. Hannah Parker, of Berkeley, California, was in attendance. Celestin's band played "Just A Closer Walk" and "The Saints" before the presentation began. City Councilman Walter M. Duffour accepted the bust on

Oscar "Papa" Celestin (1884–1954). *Courtesy of the New Orleans Jazz Club Collection of the Louisiana State Museum.*

behalf of the city with the words, "All I can say now is, God bless the soul of a wonderful old gentleman."

At the close of the dedication, the band played "Down by the Riverside."

Today, the sculpture can be seen in the Milton H. Latter branch of the New Orleans Public Library at 5120 St. Charles Avenue.

John G. Curran, a member of the New Orleans Jazz Club and a longtime friend of "Papa" Celestin, was quoted as saying, "New Orleans is lucky to have had such a good ambassador of good will. He liked to be in the south, he liked to stay in the south, mostly New Orleans. A New York agent tried to persuade 'Papa' Celestin to move to New York. 'Papa' just smiled at the man and said, 'Boss, I appreciate your interest, but they're giving away more money in New Orleans than they are making in New York.'"

Chapter 18
Two Leaders: Eddie Pierson and Sarah Celestin

1954–1958

Eddie Pierson, the trombonist with the band since 1951, was named by Sarah Celestin, "Papa's" widow, to become the musical director and on-stage leader of Celestin's Original Tuxedo Jazz Band. Pierson and "Papa" had been close, and "Papa" had actually made the decision to pass the musical leadership to Pierson. Sarah retained financial control, and as the business manager and booking agent, she made all the non-musical decisions for the band. She chose to keep the name of Celestin connected to the band to ensure continuity and protect her family's investment as she continued to collect the royalties from the recordings made while her husband was the leader.

Born in Algiers, Louisiana, on August 1, 1904, Edward "Eddie" "Red" Pierson was a grown man before he decided to learn to play the trombone. He was driving a truck for a cigar factory when he bought Steve Lewis's horn and took it to Bill Matthews's house and asked him to show him how to play the trombone. Matthews was seven or eight years older than Pierson, but they had come up together, so he agreed to teach him what he knew.

Matthews said Pierson took lessons from him for about a year and eight months, during which time he showed him where the Bb was on the horn and told him what to do and what books to use. Matthews suggested that Pierson go to Vic Gaspard or Manuel "Fess" Manetta for lessons, but Pierson preferred to get his lessons for free from Matthews and told many people later in life that Bill Matthews had taught him.

Like many other musicians, he had played on the riverboats in the 1930s and with various bands in the '40s and '50s including the Sunny South Orchestra, Armand J. Piron's Orchestra, the Young Tuxedo Brass Band, the Great Lakes Naval Station Band and the Abby Williams Happy Pals. He recorded with Herb Morand and his band in 1950 and then with Paul Barbarin and his New Orleans Jazz Band in 1951 and again in 1954.

Pierson augmented his income by teaching trombone. One of his students, Benjamin "Benny" Gordon Powell Jr., was twelve when he first started learning the trombone in the late 1940s. He later became known as a member of Lionel Hampton's and Count Basie's bands.

Shortly after the passing of Celestin, Eddie Pierson said, "We think we are doing awfully well for a leaderless band. Papa would be proud of the band today. Papa's band is good, but it will never again sparkle in the same way."

On March 17, 1956, at the WDSU radio/TV station studio on Royal Street in New Orleans, Eddie Pierson and his band recorded "The Gettysburg March," "In Gloryland" and "Bill Bailey, Won't You Please Come Home" for a compilation called *Good Time Jazz, Volume 2*.

The band members in the studio that day were Albert Walters (tp), Eddie Pierson (tb), Joseph Thomas (cl), Jeanette Kimball (p), Albert French (bj), Sidney Brown (b) and Louis Barbarin (d). They were the members of Celestin's Original Tuxedo Jazz Band, but on that day, they recorded as Pierson's band.

La Creole Fete Association de Nouvelle Orleans presented its fourth-annual open-air concert to celebrate Bastille Day on July 14, 1956. Celestin's Original Tuxedo Band had played for the first open-air concert in 1953 and every one since then. The band was hired again in 1956 to play for the festival, which was set up on the Claiborne Avenue neutral ground at Columbus Street.

The neutral ground in 1956 was a wide expanse of grass planted with four rows of oak trees that ran for blocks along that area of Claiborne Avenue. The oaks created a green canopy, which turned the area into a long shady park where families would spend time enjoying the outdoors and many planned social events. This was before the I-10's traffic-laden concrete overpass was created along that stretch of road where it traces the route of Claiborne Avenue.

Mrs. A.C. Synigal, president of the association, was there, and from the notes on her program, we know the band started at 8:00 p.m. with "Till We Meet Again." Then Joseph "Brother Cornbread" Thomas used his solo in "High Society" to get a second line going with the kids dancing behind the soft drink stand and beating on the tables with sticks.

Creole Fest, 1956. *Left to right:* Albert Walters (tp), "Cornbread" Thomas (cl), Albert French (el-g) and Larry Darnell (ent). *Courtesy of the Hogan Jazz Archive, Tulane University.*

The Master of Ceremonies, Dr. Daddy-O (Vernon Winslow), announced a gospel song, "Down By The Riverside," in memory of "Papa" Celestin. Thomas took the vocals, with Albert Fernandez Walters playing a cup mute solo on trumpet. The next tune was "That's A Plenty" with Sidney Brown playing a masterful string bass.

Jeanette Kimball and her piano had everyone dancing the Slow Drag to "The Tin Roof Blues" and "Don't Get Funky (Cause Your Water's On)." Albert Walters had a long trumpet intro to the "Bourbon Street Parade," and then Eddie Pierson kept it going with long slides on his trombone.

"Eh La Bas" featured Albert French playing the banjo. The youngsters, who had climbed into the oak trees, were shaking the limbs of the trees in time to the music and calling back to him in response.

The event ended with the band playing "The Saints," which had the crowd up on their feet, parading, dancing and jitterbugging.

An August 1957 amateur recording of Celestin's Tuxedo Jazz Band, fronted by Eddie Pierson, at a private wedding party in New Orleans was released on the Jazz Crusade Label as a compilation album, entitled *Rare Cuts—Well Done, Vol. 2.*

The band played at the groundbreaking ceremony for the new Royal Orleans Hotel at Royal and St. Louis Streets on May 14, 1958.

Eddie Pierson died seven months later, on December 17, 1958. George French, Albert's son, said, "Pierson and the band were playing music on the sidewalk in front of Generation Hall when he just fell over dead."

Chapter 19
Albert Joseph "Papa" French
1958–1977

Albert Joseph "Papa" French, the banjo player with Celestin's band since 1950, was chosen by Celestin's widow, Sarah, to become the next leader of the Original Tuxedo Jazz Band. Albert was the musical director, leader on the bandstand and also controlled the finances and bookings as Sarah Celestin had relinquished all control to him.

French was born in New Orleans on November 16, 1910, the same year that Celestin was starting to play with the band at the Tuxedo Dance Hall. His family, going back at least three generations, had always been involved with and surrounded by music. His father, Robert "Baba" French, from La Place, Louisiana, had played the brass bass, or tuba, with numerous bands around the New Orleans area. His Uncle Maurice (Morris) French played trombone, his brother John played trumpet and another uncle played the French horn.

French, in an interview with the *Times-Picayune* in July 1967, remembered that as a child of five or six years old, he was fascinated by the Saturday and Sunday dance band competitions, called bucking contests. By local custom, a dance sponsor, looking to hire a band for an event, would post advance advertisements for the competition around town. The competing bands would play on a wagon or stage at designated street corners as they vied for the job. The sponsor would watch the crowd's reaction and then choose the band that got the most applause to play for his event.

French had started playing the ukulele when he was about twelve but soon switched to the banjo and took lessons from Dave Perkins in a group band lesson for six months. Perkins had also taught Albert's father, Robert

French, to play the tuba. Within a short time, he found work with the clarinet player and bandleader Willie "Kaiser" Joseph and played in Joseph's bands for about four years in the 1920s.

Through the 1930s he worked with Eddie Jackson, a tuba player whose band had a steady gig playing jitneys every Friday, Saturday and Sunday night at a dance hall in Gretna. In the 1930s and '40s, dance halls would hire bands to play a jitney, a form of non-stop music that would go the entire night. An eight-piece band would take the stage and start playing, and after an hour, one musician would put down his instrument and leave the stage for a twenty-minute break. When his break was over, he'd return to the stage, pick up his instrument and commence playing as the next musician would put his instrument down and leave for his break. Only the drummer would always have another musician take over his instrument so as to never interrupt the beat. At the end of each individual song, the band would play a short phrase of music as they segued to the next tune so the whole time the music never stopped or even appeared to be disjointed.

In the 1940s, Albert worked with Thomas "Kid Thomas" Valentine, who Albert's son Bob has said was "an amazing trumpet player, but crazy as a betsy bug."

French soon became the leader of his own band and was playing a steady, three-night-a-week gig at Al's on Franklin Avenue. That job lasted for about five years. The men that worked in his band were Dude Lewis (tp), Albert French (bj, g), Tom Harris (b), Peter Hicks (p) and Sammy Penn (d).

French and some version of that band continued to gig around town in the evenings. French, who was married and raising a family, worked days as a carpenter building homes all over the city of New Orleans, until he was able to become a full-time musician in the late 1940s.

A bandleader would accept any job offered and occasionally double or triple book a time slot knowing there was always the possibility of a cancellation. When those cancellations didn't happen, the overbooked leader would pass the job to another bandleader and ask him to fill in. In the late 1940s, Celestin frequently asked Albert French and his band to take those extra jobs. French, with his positive, outgoing personality and his capable banjo and guitar work, was getting more popular with every job. In 1950, when Celestin needed to replace Harrison Verrett, his banjo and guitar player who had left to play with Antoine "Fats" Domino, he hired Albert French because, as Celestin was quoted as saying in a 1967 *Times-Picayune* article, "He was getting too much of my work."

More than a Century of a New Orleans Icon

Celestin's band on the Poydras Street Wharf, 1956. Albert French (bj), Louis Barbarin (d), Eddie Pierson (tb), Sidney Brown (b), Albert Walters (tp) and Adolphe Alexander (sax). *Courtesy of the Hogan Jazz Archive, Tulane University.*

In 1958, when French took over the leadership of the Tuxedo Jazz Band, he continued with a booking schedule much the same as Celestin's. He kept the band active with New Orleans society jobs, out of town dances and tours, including events at military bases. Band members continued to dress as field hands and perform on the docks of the Mississippi Shipping Company and the Delta Lines for arriving and departing cruise passengers.

As Bob French explained:

The dock was about money first. My Dad was smart about money. He would say, "You can't do anything without money." Sometimes you take shit you don't want to take. The end result is money. He could work with the biggest bull-shit artist. He could take the biggest racist and could talk to them like they were important, if they had the money. When he walked away, he had the money.

He would put the tips from the night in a paper bag and when he would get home, he would throw the money on the bed. The bed was like the kitchen counter. The whole bed would be lined up with 5's and 1's and quarters and halves.

He could hustle. He could Uncle Tommy it. He told me, "I will not go to my grave being poor." It's not a sin; it's more like its better.

Papa Celestin's Original Tuxedo Jazz Band at Dan's Pier 600, 1959. *Left to right:* Jeanette Kimball (p), Cornbread Thomas (cl), Sidney Brown (b), Albert French (bj), Albert Walters (tp), Louis Barbarin (d) and Wendell Eugene (tb). *Courtesy of the Hogan Jazz Archive, Tulane University.*

Everybody should respect the other person's "person." It's no good with no respect for yourself.

Between 1961 and 1962, the band released three vinyl albums: *Dixieland King*, *The Birth of the Blues* and *New Orleans Jazz Band*. They had been recorded in 1956 at Cosimo Matassa's studio and produced by Dave Bartholomew for Imperial Records. The band personnel on all three albums consisted of Albert Walters (tp), Eddie Pierson (tb), Joseph "Brother Cornbread" Thomas (cl), Albert French (bj), Sidney Brown (b), Octave Crosby (p) and Louis Barbarin (d).

In February 1962, the Dixieland Hall opened at 522 Bourbon Street, with seating for two hundred and standing space for another fifty to seventy-five people. The average night brought in about one hundred adults paying $1.00, with anyone twelve or younger getting in free. It wasn't intended to be a "joint" but was rather a place that welcomed all ages with an interest in experiencing the traditional jazz of New Orleans. The hall was open four nights a week from 8:30 p.m. to 12:00 a.m. and paid the musicians union scale, which was $20.50 for four hours. There was also a tip jar that added to the night's income.

The first band employed was Albert "Papa" French and the Original Tuxedo Jazz Band, and they continued to be the most popular attraction at the Dixieland Hall. His regular band consisted of Jack Willis (tp), originally from Illinois; Wendell Eugene (tb), who was a postman by day; Joseph "Brother Cornbread" Thomas, (cl) who bought his first horn for five dollars and co-wrote "Anybody Want To Buy My Cabbage" with Albert French; Jeanette Kimball (p), who was classically trained; Albert French (bj), the leader; and Louis Barbarin, who had started playing with Celestin in 1933 and, at sixty-three, was considered the fastest drummer in New Orleans.

Al Grayson Clark, the owner of Dixieland Hall, told a reporter for the *Milwaukee Sentinel* in December 1966 that on an average night, the gate would only bring in about ten dollars more than it cost him to pay the musicians. He kept the place open by recording and selling thousands of albums. Two of the most popular had been recorded on Albert French's Nobility Label: *A Night At Dixieland Hall, Vol. 1* and *A Night At Dixieland Hall, Vol. 2*, released in 1965.

Narvin Kimball started playing with Albert French's Original Tuxedo Band on out-of-town trips in 1960. He switched to upright bass, stringing his own instruments to suit the fact that he played bass as a lefty.

Bob French remembered, "Narvin and my daddy were good friends. He would come to our house, and they would play music together—Narvin on banjo and my daddy on guitar. I liked Narvin, even though he was too aggressive."

Billboard Magazine's April 13, 1963 issue had this announcement in the "Jazz Scope" column. "The New Orleans Jazz Club has resumed its Sunday afternoon Jazz Concerts. On April 28 the attraction will be the Original Celestin Tuxedo Jazz Band at the Hotel Roosevelt in New Orleans."

The band continued to travel, and in 1963, French and his Original Tuxedo Jazz Band were invited to play a four-week engagement in Naussau in the Bahamas.

The May 14, 1964 issue of *Jet Magazine* stated:

Albert "Papa" French, veteran New Orleans banjoist touring the country and appearing at the University of Minnesota in Minneapolis, declared: "Now, today, you have some interest in Dixie among the young white musicians, but the young Negro musicians are playing rock'n'roll...Part of the reason is they think Dixie is square, but it is

Albert French, circa 1965, with Louis Barbarin (d). *Courtesy of the French Family Archive.*

*also harder to play and it takes more feeling. It's got to come from the
soul, and maybe they don't feel it."*

He must have been having a bad day, because in a 1977 interview with
Claus Dahlgren for the Swedish Radio Broadcasting system and Dahlgren's
"Radio Jazz Show," French answered the question, "Are there any new
musicians coming up that keep the tradition going?"

"Oh yeah, we have a lot of young ones. In my band, we have four youngsters,
well, some of them are youngsters, the youngest is twenty-two years old. I will
keep it going because whenever an oldster gets out, I'll pull a youngster in there
to keep the music going. And I think that this music will live forever. At one
time, I was in doubt, but I think this music will go forever and ever."

The September 22, 1964 issue of the *New Orleans States-Item* had the
headline: "Tuxedo Jazz Band headed to the Berlin Jazz Festival," as the band
left on a lengthy tour of venues in Switzerland, Sweden, Denmark, France
and Germany.

More than a Century of a New Orleans Icon

The December 1964 issue of *Jazz Monthly* had a review by Ken Palmer of the October 3, 1964 concert that took place at the Johanneshovs Isstadion in Stockholm and was billed as "the USA Jazz Festival." He wrote:

> *It was even more remarkable to find the Original Tuxedo Jazz Band were the biggest hit of the evening. Albert French on banjo introduced Joseph "Brother Cornbread" Thomas, clarinet; Joshua F. Willis, trumpet; Joseph Watkins, trombone; Waldren "Frog" Joseph, trombone; Frank Fields, string bass; Louis Barbarin, drums and on piano Jeanette Kimball. What had the audience stamping and cheering was not only their playing, but unlike all the others that came before and after them they used a vaudeville routine. Their repertoire ranged from "Panama Rag" to "Wolverine Blues" and when the band swung into "Mama Don't Allow" it proved to be one of the two memorable spots, with Albert French sticking his banjo behind his left ear and turning round and round in circles to show the folks the art of playing behind your back. The other spot was "old man" "Cornbread" playing his own composition, "Eh La Bas," and in between playing, continually hoisting his unintentionally slipping trousers. The band seemed held together by the great Louis Barbarin, whilst Jeanette Kimball's playing was also outstanding.*

There was a recording made during the 1964 European trip and released as the Original Tuxedo Jass Band. The tunes on it include: "Just a Closer Walk With Thee"; "Oh Didn't He Ramble"; "The World is Waiting for the Sunrise"; "Eh! La Bas," with Joseph "Brother Cornbread" Thomas on clarinet; "Panama," with Wendell Eugene on trombone; "Tin Roof Blues"; and "Original Dixieland One Step."

That Wendell Eugene was recorded on trombone on one of the cuts points out that it was not uncommon for the lineup to change as some players would fly home and others would fly to Europe to replace them. The AFM maintained guidelines for the number of musicians a band was required to have for each job. Union musicians working union jobs had contracts that specified the number of musicians working for each gig, and they had to be honored.

The June 5, 1966 edition of the *Courier-Journal* remarked:

> *Pete Fountain's French Quarter Inn on Bourbon Street was charging a $4.50 cover to go in and listen to 3 sets of music in a modern décor while*

sitting on upholstered seats. Al Hirt's place was featuring vaudeville acts and comedians while Hirt was touring on the road with his band. Dixieland Hall, 522 Bourbon Street, a pristine old jazz hall with paintings carefully placed over patches on the wall was where he found 64 year old Louis Barbarin on the drums and Jeanette Kimball playing clean ragtime on the upright. It's a small place where 60 people is a packed house. Preservation Hall, a block away in a rickety building, had standing room only for their 35 minute sets. Emma Barrett with little to the music except nostalgia was in her trademark red skull-cap over her short, curly hair and wearing a garter with jingling bells attached around her ankle.

"Sweet" Emma Barrett, also known as "The Bell Gal," was a piano playing legend in New Orleans. Mrs. Steve Valenti, whose husband owned the Paddock, suggested to Emma that she wear the bells around her ankles or knees to attract attention. She had played with Celestin's Tuxedo Jazz Band and then had gone with Ridgley after the Celestin/Ridgley split in the early 1920s.

In the late 1960s, the French family was living in a house Albert had built at 1218 Robert Street, and Emma Barrett was close by in the Gert Town

"Sweet" Emma Barrett, circa 1960. *Courtesy of the Hogan Jazz Archive, Tulane University.*

area. Emma had a stroke in 1967 and lost some mobility, so Albert delegated his son Bob to go to her home, help her to the car and drive her to his gig. Bob remembers her as being "ornery with a lack of class. She would always have a small brown paper bag with a sandwich in it so she could eat without having to leave the piano bench."

One night, on the break, while she was sitting at her piano eating her sandwich a tourist approached her and tried unsuccessfully to engage her in a conversation. He didn't receive a response but continued talking. Finally, he thought he was making some progress when, without looking up, she asked him, "Where are you from?"

"Germany," he replied.

"Go back there."

THE *NEW ORLEANS TIMES-PICAYUNE* had a short report in the July 30, 1967 issue that declared "Papa" Albert French and his Original Tuxedo Jazz Band still had four original members of "Papa" Celestin's Original Tuxedo Band, namely: Albert French, Jeanette Salvant Kimball, Joseph "Brother Cornbread" Thomas and Louis Barbarin. The newer members were Frank Fields, bass; Jack Willis, trumpet; and Wendell Eugene, trombone.

The year 1968 was the first year of the Hampton Jazz Festival at the Hampton Institute in Virginia. The Original Tuxedo Jazz Band was one of the bands featured in the program "The Roots of Jazz," which was meant not only to be musical but also educational, with French following the Staple Singers and preceeding the Muddy Waters Blues Band.

The August 31, 1969 issue of the *Times-Picayune* reported that "Jazz on Sunday Afternoon," which had been postponed by Hurricane Camille, would be taking place in the Grand Salon of the Royal Orleans Hotel. The band would be "Papa" French and the former Celestin's Tuxedo Jazz Orchestra, with special guest Emma Barrett on piano. Tickets were available at Werlein's music store for $2.50 or would be available at the door for $3.00.

"Sweet" Emma Barrett frequently played with the Tuxedo Band at Dixieland Hall, but she also played with ensembles of her own compilation and with the Preservation Hall Jazz Band. It was a well-known fact that she was out of her house every night, and knowing how rough it was in the neighborhood where she lived, it was no surprise when she returned home one night and found someone had broken into her house and stolen her money.

Bob French said, "She had those old ideas about keeping her money under the mattress. When she told us about the robbery, she said they didn't get it all cause she had some at another place in the house. She wouldn't say where, but a few nights later, the thieves went back and took the rest of it." *Down Beat* magazine reported on May 27, 1971:

> *Scale increase kills New Orleans Dixieland Hall; New Orleans' Dixieland Hall closed its doors April 12 after a ten-year run on Bourbon Street.*
>
> *The closing followed on the heels of the recent wage for union musicians. The raise in scale was approved by members of Local 174-496 in a close election. Reportedly, members playing at Dixieland Hall and other New Orleans locations featuring traditional music voted heavily against the increase.*
>
> *A severe turndown in business due to the recession plus the increase in scale proved too much for the management of the hall, which had been running at a recent $10,000 annual deficit.*
>
> *Albert "Papa" French and the Original Tuxedo Jazz Band with "Sweet" Emma Barrett were hired to play the final night at Dixieland Hall.*

Bob French, who was already a member of the Tuxedo Jazz Band when Dixieland Hall closed, says he disagreed with that bit of reporting. "Most musicians playing traditional, or trad, jazz did vote for the increase. Who wouldn't? It was a pay raise for us.

"Before Louisiana became a 'Right to Work' state, you had to be a Union member to be hired, and the Union set the pay scale, which dictated the minimum wage you could be paid. My daddy usually played for more than scale. It all depended on the contract he'd make with the club owner."

With Dixieland Hall closing, a lot of people thought the future of traditional New Orleans jazz might be not so bright. Albert French was more optimistic, as the *New Orleans Times-Picayune* learned when he was interviewed about the early days of Storyville for its August 29, 1971 "Dixie" section. The story was entitled, "Jazz Immortals Reminisce":

> *Most of the guys were working around Storyville in those days and you couldn't say they were making any money. Most of them had regular daytime jobs. Still, when they got off work in the morning, they'd go down to "The Entertainers" on Iberville and jam. They'd also have jam sessions at the Tick Tock, the Roof Garden the Pelican Club and…oh, so many places that aren't open now.*

We played the speakeasies through prohibition, but we weren't making any money. I played at one speakeasy for 4 years—Friday, Saturday and Sunday—and it never got raided. The owner was just lucky I guess.

There were a lot of legitimate dance halls around, too. Jazz bands would get on the back of a truck and ride through the streets playing their music to advertise the dance halls. Yeah, they were legitimate, but people always found a way to bring the bootleg liquor in with them.

When prohibition broke a lot of beer parlors started opening up and so we began branching out. Bourbon Street didn't really exist then, but there were clubs all over the quarter. The Caliente Club on Dauphine, The Dog House on Rampart and Conti. There were things around. That was before we had a musicians union. If you wanted to work, you had to work until the proprietor told you that you could stop. I played at the jitney dances where the girls worked for a dime a dance. And it was pretty bad. We played from 8:00 at night until 8:30 the next morning. That's how bad it was. So, in a way, I'd have to say things are a lot better for musicians now than they used to be.

My sons, Bob and George, are playing with the Storyville Jazz Band. They're working out like crazy and that's pretty good. That's pretty nice. And other musician's sons are going in for jazz, too. Frog Joseph's is playing trombone and Jack Willis' is playing trumpet, I think. So, I don't think Rock n Roll is going to replace Dixieland. The future looks pretty good; pretty fair.

The *New Orleans Times-Picayune* kept everyone informed as to the locations where the Tuxedo Band would be playing. The May 23, 1971 issue reported, "Papa Albert French and the Papa Celestin Tuxedo Orchestra featuring 'Sweet Emma Barrett' will be at the Grand Ballroom at the Royal Sonesta Hotel on May 30. The band members include Jack Willis [tp], Joseph 'Brother Cornbread' Thomas [cl], Homer Eugene [tb], Jeanette Kimball [p], Frank "Dude" Fields [b], Louis Barbarin [d] and 'Papa' French [bj].

"They will feature, on piano and vocals, Emma Barrett who had started to work for Celestin at 12 years old. She can't read music, has worked for many top jazz bands and is a favorite of jazz buffs for her piano and her vocalizing."

The *New Orleans States-Item* of October 21, 1971, reported that the Jazz in Jackson Square program, sponsored by the New Orleans Recreation Department (NORD) and the Musicians Union Locals 174 and 496, would have "Papa" Albert French and the Original Tuxedo Band and Leo Nocentelli

Albert French's Original Tuxedo Jazz Band, 1971. *Left to right:* Bob French (d), Jeanette Kimball (p), Cornbread Thomas (cl), Albert French (bj), Clive Wilson (tp), Homer Eugene (tb) and Frank Fields (b). *Courtesy of the Hogan Jazz Archive, Tulane University.*

and the Meters headline the last two concerts of the season. The St. Augustine High School Band joined them at the last concert on October 30.

French and the band were booked every year for a number of the popular Jazz in Jackson Square programs. Bob French said that the band would sometimes start at Crazy Shirley's Club, a popular music club at Bourbon and St. Peter Streets in the French Quarter, and lead a second line from there to Jackson Square, a short two-and-a-half-block walk. There were two boys, about ten and eleven years old, who would bring their cornet and clarinet and march with the band. When they got to Jackson Square, the young boys, Wynton and Branford Marsalis, would beg to be allowed to step up and play on the bandstand with the band. "Papa" would let them, and the crowd loved it. The problem was, between the crowd wanting more and the kids not wanting to stop, he'd have a hard time getting them to step down.

Encouraging the development of young musicians was a concern for French, as it continues to be for all bandleaders in the city. For traditional New Orleans music and the New Orleans music tradition to continue, young musicians have to be nurtured. This happens at home, among their contemporaries and in the schools. Albert never missed an opportunity to spread the "music gospel" to the next generation.

The New Orleans Times-Picayune of December 3, 1971, reported:

> *The Jazz in education Program for the NOLA Public Schools, financed by the School Office of Cultural Resources and The Louisiana Jazz Club through grants from the National Endowment for the Arts and the Louisiana Music Therapy Fund, has hired three jazz artists, Papa French banjoist, Armand Hug pianist and Dave Oxley drummer to perform a concert and inspire the students as they try to start a band at the Milne Boys' Home. The school will pay for the concert. J. Durel Black, of the jazz club, said the fund will provide the instruments and the music teachers will come from the public school system. The program is headed by Shirley Trusty.*

Information for the New Orleans Jazz and Heritage Festival to be held from Wednesday, April 26, through Sunday, April 30, was released on February 3, 1972.

"The [Jazz and Heritage] foundation has sponsored two previous festivals," Arthur Q. Davis, president of the foundation, said with the release. Admission to the fairgrounds for the midway, which was a three-day fair of native crafts and produce with food concessions during the day, cost two dollars for adults and one dollar for students and children. The night performances were in the International Room at the Fairmont Hotel, the Ballroom of the Jung Hotel, the Municipal Auditorium and the steamer *President*.

The Tuxedo Band had performed at both of the previous Jazz and Heritage Festivals, and for this year's fest, French and the band were booked for April 26 on the SS *President*, with Pete Fountain being the featured performer for that evening. Tickets for the nighttime performances were $4.50, $5.50 or $6.50 for events in the auditorium, $5.50 for each hotel event and $5.00 for each event aboard the SS *President*.

On Monday, May 15, 1972, "French and the band were at the Plimsoll Club Lounge for 'A Night of New Orleans Jazz' presented by the Louisiana Jazz Club. Some of the tunes played that night were; 'Bill Bailey Won't You Please Come Home,' 'Bourbon Street Parade,' 'Basin Street Blues' and 'The Saints,'" according to the *New Orleans States-Item*.

In a letter dated December 12, 1972, Richard B. Allen described coming on a second-line "parade from Jackson Square to Crazy Shirley's." The Olympia Brass band was parading, though "Albert French's band was doing most of the playing," with extra musicians joining in as they walked. Allen commented, "Clive Wilson sounded good on trumpet." Joseph "Brother Cornbread" Thomas was there marching and playing the clarinet even though the event was a benefit for him, as he was "due to go into the hospital the next day with possible bladder troubles."

In April 1973, Heritage Hall opened at 516 Bourbon Street in the French Quarter. Originally named Dixieland Hall, it was founded by Grayson Clark in 1961 at a different location and then moved to 516 Bourbon in 1962, where it was a popular jazz club until economic conditions forced it to close in 1971.

Heritage Hall had a flyer to announce the opening of its Creole Kitchen in 1974. Just drinks—no food—with regular draught beer priced at $0.45, wine by the glass at $0.60, highballs or super draught beer at $0.95, call brands at $1.10, hurricanes in a souvenir glass at $2.50 and the house special, a Moscow Mule, a combination of vodka and ginger beer that was served in a souvenir mug for $2.00. All this, plus "Evening Concerts of Authentic New Orleans Music."

The September 15, 1973 issue of the *States-Item* reported that for the month of September, "Papa" French and the band would be performing nightly (except Monday), from 9:30 p.m. to 1:30 a.m., at the Fairmont Court in the Fairmont (previously the Roosevelt) Hotel. Blanche Thomas had joined the band as a vocalist.

In a letter dated March 1974, Richard B. Allen noted that the band consisted of Clive Wilson (tp), Homer Eugene (tb), Clarence Ford (cl), "Papa" French (bj), Jeanette Kimball (p) and Bob French (d).

Bob French tells the story of how their band of black musicians, dressed in perfectly tailored tuxedos, was expected to approach their workplace at the Fairmont. They would carry their instruments, including the upright bass, past the front entrance of the Fairmont Hotel and walk around the corner, picking their way through the greasy trash and garbage area, complete with roaches and "rats as big as dogs" to enter the building through the kitchen door. On their first night, as the band walked past the hotel's entrance, Jeanette Kimball, a Creole with a light complexion who was able to pass as white, split from the group and went straight through the main door as the rest of the astonished band watched. When questioned later she said, "I am not walking past all that garbage while I'm wearing a $200.00 dress." And she never did.

The Wednesday, March 20, 1974 issue of *Figaro* had a sample listing of who was playing locally. Papa Albert French and the Tuxedo Jazz Band were in the Blue Room at the Fairmont, a step up from the Fairmont Court, from 9:30 p.m. to 1:30 a.m., with a $2.00 cover charge. Ray Charles was playing there with a $12.00 cover during the week and $15.00 on the weekend. Over at the Maple Leaf on Oak Street, the Society Jazz Band could be heard for free. At Sylvia's, at 4612 Freret, the Del Rays were playing on Sundays from 10:00 p.m. to 2:00 a.m., with no cover and no drink minimum. On the steamer *President*, moored at the foot of Canal Street, the Frank Frederico Band was playing Dixieland and standards while cruising the Mississippi River from 8:30 p.m. until midnight with a charge of $4.00. The 544 Club on Bourbon Street had the C.J. Cheramie Trio, no cover charge, but a one-drink ($1.55) minimum.

According to the *Times-Picayune* of August 25, 1974, the final 1974 concert for the Jazz in the Afternoon series, which was presented every year by the New Orleans Jazz Club, took place in the Mardi Gras Room at the Marriott Hotel on Sunday, August 25. Papa Albert French and the Tuxedo Jazz Band with Clive Wilson (tp), Homer Eugene (tb), "Brother Cornbread" Thomas (cl), Papa French (bj), Frank Fields (b), Jeanette Kimball (p) and Bob French (d) was the band chosen to close out the season.

The *States-Item* of September 17, 1974, reported that the Tuxedo Jazz Band continued to be the band hired for most society events. In September, "Papa," with his usual seven-piece lineup, played during the champagne luncheon that preceded a Fur Fashion Show held in the International Room of the Fairmont Hotel.

This seven-piece configuration of the band had become standard, though it could vary depending on a musician's schedule or if there was interest in having a special guest performer. The *New Orleans Times-Picayune* for December 14, 1974, reported that trumpeter Wallace Davenport was a special guest with "Papa" and the Original Tuxedo Jazz Band when they played a benefit for the Crippled Children's Hospital at LaGallerie in the Marriott Hotel.

The Fairmont Hotel had a number of rooms where entertainment was available, and on one particular night in the early 1970s, the Dick Stabile Band was in the Blue Room while the Original Tuxedo Jazz Band was in the Fairmont Court. The musicians from both bands were outside smoking on their break, but French didn't like what Stabile's band was smoking, so he told his men to stay away from the cluster of them standing by the back entrance to the Orpheum. The Tuxedo's trumpet player that night, James May, ignored French, found his way over and shared a smoke. When the break was over, French confronted May and told him, "Go over again and I'll fire you." May replied, "Fuck you."

French grabbed for May, who took off with French in pursuit. He chased May across Canal Street, dodging traffic. May's coattails were straight out behind him in the wind, and French got one hand on them, but May slipped out of his coat and kept running until he reached the neutral ground in the middle of the street, where the streetcar tracks were side by side. By then, Bob French and a cab driver had caught Papa French and were holding him while they tried to calm him down. The whole time, May never ceased calling French a slew of dirty names, and he didn't stop until Bob had enough and shouted at him, "You son of a bitch, go home before I turn my daddy loose on you."

May left muttering and disappeared into the French Quarter. When the band returned to the bandstand, they found May's horn sitting there. Bob got the horn back to May with the help of a third party. As Bob tells the rest of the story, "May is now playing on the Moonwalk hustling tourists. If I'm doing so much wrong, why am I driving a Cadillac and he's peddling a bike and going to the two-dollar window?"

Paul Lentz's Heritage Hall, at 605 St. Anne Street on the corner at Jackson Square, reopened on Friday, September 27, 1974, and had "Papa" French and the Original Tuxedo Jazz Band and the Louis Cottrell Band as two of the regular bands there. Richard B. Allen notated in a letter dated October 1974 that Clive Wilson, originally from England and the trumpet player for the Tuxedo, had told him that business had been good since the reopening.

A 1975 flyer from Heritage Hall listed admission for adults as $1.50 and children $1.00, with daily performances featuring the New Orleans Joymakers from 12:30 p.m. to 5:30 p.m. Evening performances were from 8:30 p.m. to 12:30 a.m. nightly. The bands under contract at that time were Louis Cottrell's Heritage Hall Jazz Band; Blanche Thomas, "Queen of the Blues"; Albert "Papa" French and his Original Tuxedo Jazz Band; Danny Barker's New Orleans Jazz Hounds; and the Onward Brass Band.

Papa French and his wife, Claudia Samuel French, opened Tradition Hall at 721 Bourbon Street in 1975. It was an all-ages kind of place where the focus was on traditional New Orleans jazz. There was a "donation" of $1.50 for adults or $1.00 for kids at the door, and the first set started at 8:30 p.m. Between sets, a jazz aficionado could buy a soda from the vending machines and choose from a selection of albums featuring local jazz bands. The live music was either French and his band or the Louis Cottrell Band. Occasionally another band would fill in if both French's and Cottrell's bands were traveling, but the music was always traditional New Orleans jazz.

More than a Century of a New Orleans Icon

Tradition Hall, circa 1975. Freddy Lonzo (tb), Wendell Brunious (tp), Frank Fields (b), Donald Suhor (cl), Bob French (d) and Albert French (bj). *Courtesy of the French Family Archive.*

While a lot of bands (even today in New Orleans) will let outside musicians come up from the audience and sit in, that wasn't the norm for Tradition Hall. It was more of a showcase for the traditional jazz as played by the bands in residence—with one exception. Soon after Tradition Hall opened, eight-year-old Harry Connick Jr. would show up almost every Saturday night and spend a little time being a kid, playing on the sidewalk and climbing the light poles in front of the building. When he got inside, the band would let him sit in with them and play one of the tunes he knew on the piano. Bob French said, "We'd have to go out there and yell, 'Boomer, come in off those posts!' We knew he had talent and now he is one of the 'baddest' piano players in the world."

In April 1975, the Tuxedo Jazz Band recorded two LPs on its own Second Line label. The band consisted of Clive Wilson (tp), Homer Eugene (tb), "Brother Cornbread" Thomas (cl, voc), "Papa" Albert French (bj, voc), Frank Fields (b), Jeanette Kimball (p) and Bob French (d).

The first album was *Albert "Papa" French and the Original Tuxedo Jazz Band, Vol. 1,* and the second was *Albert "Papa" French at Tradition Hall, Vol. 2.* Both albums were produced by Bob French and engineered by Skip Godwin, with assistance from Dave Bartholomew and Jayne Wood.

In May 1975, Papa French and the band played for the Creole Fiesta Association Ball. The band consisted of Clive Wilson (tp), Jack Willis (tp), Homer Eugene (tb), "Brother Cornbread" Thomas (cl, voc), Albert French (bj, voc), Frank Fields (b), Jeanette Kimball (p) and Smokey Johnson (d). A 1975 letter from Richard B. Allen says, "Wilson, Willis and Eugene also harmonized on some of the songs and danced."

The band played at a reception for King Hussein of Jordan in May, and on June 15, 1975, the New Orleans Jazz Club presented Jazz on Sunday Afternoon from 3:00 to 5:00 p.m. at the Marriott Hotel, with French and the Original Tuxedo Jazz Band playing for their fourteenth straight year. Tickets for the concert were $3.50 in advance at Werlein's Music Store and the Jazz Museum at 833 Conti Street or $4.00 at the door.

In a letter dated March 15, 1976, from Richard B. Allen, he reported that on the previous Sunday, he had listened to "Papa" French's band at Jackson Square. In addition to the regular band, the lineup that day included Dave Bartholomew (tp), Fred Lonzo (tb) and Ellis Marsalis (el-p).

On July 4, 1976, the day that Louis Armstrong would have turned seventy-six, New Orleans celebrated with a Louis Armstrong birthday party in Jackson Square, sponsored by NORD's Cultural Division and by the American Federation of Musicians Local 174–496. The day featured music by the Alvin Alcorn Jazz Band, Danny Barker's Jazz Hounds and Albert French and the Original Tuxedo Jazz Band.

French and the band led the parade of people who made their way through the square to the site where the statue of Louis Armstrong was unveiled. The sculpture has since been moved to its permanent home inside Louis Armstrong Park.

French and the band played a regular weekly gig at the Hall of Jazz, (the old Heritage Hall) at 605 St. Anne Street. The Hall of Jazz also featured performances by Louis Cottrell and his band, Blanche Thomas and Lloyd Washington (from the Ink Spots) and billed itself as "The Home of Traditional Jazz." There were nightly performances from 8:30 p.m. to 12:30 a.m.

Albert "Papa" French passed suddenly on Wednesday, September 28, 1977. Survivors included his wife, Claudia Samuel French; two brothers, Ernest and Harold French; one sister, Cesla Maxan; three sons, George, Robert and Albert French; eleven grandchildren; and one great-grandchild. Another sister, Alberta Johnson, had passed earlier.

Albert French and the Original Tuxedo Jazz Band, 1977. Bob French (d), Frank Fields (b), Jeanette Kimball (p), Donald Suhor (cl), "Papa" Albert French (bj), Wendell Brunious (tp) and Freddie Lonzo (tb). *Courtesy of the Hogan Jazz Archive, Tulane University.*

The funeral service was held on Friday, October 1, 1977, at Our Lady of Lourdes Catholic Church at 4423 LaSalle Street, New Orleans. Narvin Kimball played "What a Friend We Have in Jesus" as a banjo solo at the service.

Musicians from French's Tuxedo Jazz Band and Louis Cottrell's band played him home as his coffin left the church. He is buried in the St. James Cemetery in La Place, Louisiana.

On Sunday, October 30, 1977, there was a memorial for Albert French held in Jackson Square. The people of New Orleans came out in droves to pay their respects to an extremely popular bandleader who had become known around the world for his commitment to the traditional music of New Orleans. The French brothers, George and Bob, brought their bands and performed together on a stage erected at Jackson Square. George led his Storyville Jazz Band, with Teddy Riley (tp), Waldren "Frog" Joseph (tb), Otis Bazoon (cl), George French (el-b) and Emile Vinette (el-p). Bob led the Original Tuxedo Jazz Band, with Wendell Brunious (tp), Scotty Hill (tb), "Brother Cornbread" Thomas (guest cl), Don Suhor (cl, sax), Emmanual Sayles (bj), Frank Fields (b), Ellis Marsalis (el-p), Bob French (ldr, d) and Germaine Bazzle (voc).

Chapter 20

Robert Thomas "Bob" French Sr.

1977–2011

A fter his death, the leadership of the band passed, as Albert French requested, to the band's drummer, his middle son, Bob French.

Robert Thomas "Bob" French was born on December 27, 1937, in New Orleans, Louisiana, the son of Albert and Claudia Samuel French. He was raised in a home on Telemaccus Street that was continually full of music and musicians.

I remember those dudes when I was three or four cause they were always there. They were like a second family. Father Al Lewis played guitar, banjo and sang and was a piece of material. He was the nicest man in the world. He and my daddy were very tight. He and my daddy, every now and then, he'd come in the house, got the bottle in his hand. Bring it in the back. He'd fix him a drink and fix my daddy a drink. The house was like here, living room, dining room then you go out in the kitchen. The kitchen has swinging doors. My mama locked the swinging doors, and she closed the other doors in the middle of the house and they got it. See, in other words, they're not going to interfere with the whole house. Her kitchen is sane, ok, and the rest of the house is sane. And they're gonna play for hours. The more they drink the more they played. Mama didn't care. I never heard my mama say one time you all been playing long enough. My mama wasn't stupid. That was her bread and butter. My mama loved music.

Early on, Bob decided he would be a drummer. His father thought he might make a better choice and explained to his son that a drummer is the first to arrive at a gig with the most equipment to set up and the last to leave with the most equipment to break down. He even went so far as to buy Bob a new King trumpet.

Bob tried the trumpet but was determined to play the drums. Without telling his father, Bob went to Louis Barbarin, whom he considers the greatest drummer of all times, for lessons. Bob said, "Louis Barbarin was the king, and his brother, Paul, was right there beside him. I really admired both men. There are none greater in modern music or jazz."

Eventually, Albert acknowledged the inevitable and went with Bob to a pawnshop, where he paid $110.00 for a set of second-hand Premiere drums for his son.

In 1952, at the age of fifteen, with his new driver's license, Bob was hired by "Papa" Celestin to drive the band to gigs using the old school bus Celestin had fitted out as a tour bus. If the band was going on the road, Bob would drive a loop around town, stopping at each musician's home to load him and his equipment.

As he remembered, "Wendell Eugene lived the farthest away and was the last to be picked up. One afternoon when we got to his house, his daughter was there with him. The little girl looked up at the bus and said, 'You'll never make it.' Celestin called her that the rest of his life."

While a student in St. Augustine High School, Bob organized his first rhythm and blues band during the 1951–52 school year. The members named the band the Turquoise and started practicing together, and soon they were playing around the city, mostly at high school dances. They did have one slight problem—the mother of their fifteen-year-old piano player wouldn't let her son go on any of the nighttime gigs.

As Bill Grady, staff reporter for the *Times-Picayune* reported the story:

> *He was really good with an almost unnatural ear for music. The Turquoise had to have him, so they went to his home near Shakespeare Park on La Salle Street and knocked on his mother's door. She opened it to find the entire band—Bob French, Art Neville, Charles Neville, J.C. Goodes and Cyrus Cagnolatti—looking up at her.*
>
> *"We'll make sure James gets back home all right, Mrs. Booker," one of them said. And that's how James Booker became one of The Turquoise.*

"Booker was the brains," Bob said when talking about that first band. "We'd all start playing something, and he'd yell, 'No, no, that's wrong.' Then he'd show us the correct way." The band lasted a short while before Art Neville was recruited by the Hawkettes as a singer; James Booker left and played with everybody in town. Bob, vocalist James "Sugar Boy" Crawford and bassist Erving Charles got together and called themselves the Commodores. They booked enough gigs that Bob was a musician by night and a student by day. He wore sunglasses in the classroom to hide the dark circles under his eyes from the late hours he was keeping. He admitted they also came in handy when he fell asleep in class.

Because most musicians like to have more than one band, Bob put together the next incarnation of the Turquoise, which included Sammy Alcorn (tp), James Rivers (sax), Kidd

Bob French, circa 1954. *Courtesy of the French Family Archive.*

Jordan (sax), George Davis (el-b, as), Alvin "Shine" Robinson (g), George French (b) and Bob French (d). According to Bob, "If you heard Alvin sing, you heard Ray Charles. He could do a perfect imitation of Ray Charles. He was that good. He got the name 'Shine' for the way the sun would bounce off his forehead."

By the mid- to late 1950s, the bands were playing more than just high school dances. They would take the Jackson Street Ferry to play in the Joy Lounge, a segregated club on New Orleans' West Bank. It was Italian-owned, and while they had to go in the back door and through the kitchen, there was always a fifth of liquor on their table when they got there. Before they took to the stage, they would order a meal, and it would be hot and on the table for them when they took their break.

They were also traveling around Louisiana. There was a club in Donaldsonville named the Town and Country Club, owned by Tony Fuesetter and his brother, where Bob and Sugar Boy's band was hired to play on Friday and Saturday nights. Once or twice a month, they'd pile all their instruments and themselves into two cars to make the trip. They'd play all night and then sleep, mosquitoes and all, in the cars because there were no hotels for blacks in town. When they arrived for the gig one night, Sugar Boy's car was in bad shape after being in an accident. One of the Fuesetter brothers saw it, and the next week when they arrived to play, there was a brand-new car sitting there. The club owners took Sugar Boy over to it and handed him the keys.

By the late 1950s, Bob was getting regular work around New Orleans when Earl Palmer, the studio drummer that had played for every band in the city, left to find work in California. Palmer had fallen in love with a white woman, and they were able to get married in California, but not in New Orleans, where her father was a police officer. Bob started getting calls to take Palmer's place on various studio jobs.

The person most instrumental in getting Bob more work as a studio drummer was Dave Bartholomew. Dave had been composing music and playing trumpet since Celestin's time and is related to Bob on his mother's side of the family. He called Bob one morning and told him to get to Cosimo Matassa's recording studio to play with Antoine "Fats" Domino because his regular drummer had not shown up.

> *I was laying around watching TV when he called. Twenty minutes later I was dressed, in the studio, and the drums were set up ready to play.*
>
> *We finished the first take of the first song and Fats said, "Play it back." Dave listened and said, "That sounds good." Fats said, "Take another one." We did twenty-two takes of that one song, twenty-two takes, I'll never forget it. We were on the clock and after each play back Fats would want another take. Clarence Ford looked over at me and laughed, "This is your first time, man. Sit your ass down. You're in for a surprise." After the twenty-second take, Dave asked Fats to play back the first take again. After he listened to it, Fats said "That's it." We didn't care because when you're on the clock and you go past three hours, the money goes way up. After the session, Fats told Dave to "Hire that boy for all my recordings." I had steady work with Fats, first at Matassa's [recording studio] and later at the studio Fats built on his property in the Ninth Ward. Fats would have a case of beer and a fifth of scotch sitting on the piano. Lee Allen, the saxophone player, was the only one, other than Fats, who could touch it.*

Later, Fats wanted to hire Bob to be part of the touring band, but Dave told him not to do it. "He'll pay you $400 a week, but he'll give you $2,000 worth of trouble."

Fats Domino may have been a national sensation who had musically crossed racial lines, but the other bands still had to deal with segregation, which continued to be an issue in this country. There was a whites-only club in Thibodeaux, Louisiana, where the stage for the band was surrounded by a wooden-framed chicken wire partition. A policeman was stationed at the base of the stage, but his job wasn't so much to protect the band as it was to keep the white women away from the black musicians. These musicians were good-looking, talented guys, so it's no surprise the women were interested and would try to pass notes with all kinds of offers through the chicken wire. If it was anything other than a request for a song, the guard would just rip it up.

The year 1961 found Bob stationed with the army in Augusta, Georgia. When he returned home to New Orleans in 1965, he picked up his drumsticks and got back to playing R&B every night with Clarence "Frogman" Henry at the 544 Club on Bourbon Street, making about $500 a week. He did some freelancing around town and was spending more time as a session man in the studio with Dave Bartholomew.

One night in 1965, Louis Barbarin, the regular drummer for the Tuxedo Band, was sick and couldn't make the gig. That night changed Bob's life forever.

My dad came into my room and said, "Put on your blue suit, you're playing with us tonight." Talk about a rude awakening. "Bourbon Street Parade" was the only thing I knew. But I went on the gig. He had a hell of a band. By the end of the night, I found out how much I didn't know about music...From that day on I respected traditional jazz."

When I started working with the band I got some good advice from Louis Barbarin about playing the drums. He told me to just relax and said, "You don't have to play all over the drums. Just keep the beat." He told me when you get to a solo, play whatever you want to.

When I played with my dad, I felt like I was king of the world. My dad could play, tell you what. He'd be home by 11:00 a.m. to sleep. He'd be up by 6:00 p.m., and he'd lay his clothes out. My mom would come in the room and would straighten out any poor clothing choices, then he'd put his clothes on in front of a mirror. He was very meticulous.

Bob was getting more involved with traditional jazz and played with the Storyville Jazz Band at Crazy Shirley's for a run of about six years, from 1965 to 1971. That band included Teddy Riley (tp), Freddy Lonzo or Scott Hil (tb), Otis Bazoon (cl), George French (b), Ellis Marsalis (p) and Bob French (ldr, d). He also was a fill-in drummer with Frank Assunto and the

Dukes of Dixieland. In 1971, he became the regular drummer for "Papa" French and the Original Tuxedo Jazz Band.

In 1977, with the passing of "Papa" French, there was a short-lived dispute as to who was going to actually lead the band. French had requested the leadership of the band be passed to his son, Bob, the Tuxedo's drummer. Bob didn't aggressively pursue new bookings for the band, and soon Clive Wilson, the Englishman who had played trumpet with "Papa" French, was going around town telling everyone he was the new Tuxedo bandleader. He

Original Tuxedo Jazz Band at Tradition Hall, 1979. *Left to right.* Freddy Lonzo (tb), Chris Burke (cl), Ed Frank (p), Bob French (d), Wendell Brunious (tp) and Joe Payton (b). *Courtesy of the French Family Archive.*

had gotten Jeanette Kimball and Frank Fields to go with him and was trying to book some work. Placide Adams, a snare drum player with the Onward Brass Band, told his friend Bob what was going on, and Bob immediately got serious about being the leader of the Original Tuxedo Jazz Band. He confronted Clive, who backed away from the idea of leading the band when Bob told him, "I'll put an ass whipping on you that no one will take off."

Bob French's Original Tuxedo Jazz Band went into the 1980s with an assemblage of some of the best traditional jazz musicians the city had to offer. On trumpet was Wendell Brunious, who had played with "Papa" French, and Teddy Riley, who came over from the Storyville band. On trombone, French had Freddy Lonzo, whom Bob considers the best traditional jazz trombone player in the city, and Scotty Hill, who had learned to play from "Frog" Joseph, both from the Storyville band. Don Suhor, also from the Storyville Band, played saxophone, and on occasion, he would pull out the clarinet, though that was not a regular part of the line. The banjo was also not a regular part of the line, but Emmanuel Sayles would sit in with the band occasionally. Frank Fields continued with the Tuxedo Band on bass, and Jeanette Kimball stayed and played piano with the band until the early

Touring France, March 1972. Frank Fields (b), Bob French (d), Wendell Brunious (tp) and Freddy Lonzo (tb). *Courtesy of the French Family Archive.*

1990s, when she retired from music. Bob had command of the microphone and led the band from behind the drum set.

His rules were simple and much the same as his father's.

> *1. Every band member is expected to be on the job and ready to play at fifteen minutes to the hour.*
>
> *2. Dress code is blue or black suit or tuxedo unless otherwise informed...no tennis shoes...no jeans...no exceptions.*
>
> *3. Intermissions are fifteen minutes. Return to the bandstand promptly without me looking for you or calling for you.*
>
> *4. If you need to reschedule a performance that you already have on your calendar that you had confirmed with me you must give me two weeks advance notice in writing.*
>
> *5. Any questions call me.*

Chapter 21
Recording and Touring and New Orleans

In 1977, Bob took the band into the Ultra Sonic Studios in New Orleans, where they recorded and released The *Tuxedo Jazz Band at Tradition Hall, Volume III* on their own Second Line label. In 1978, he recorded and released *Bob French and the Original Storyville Jazz Band* on the Second Line label. The other release in 1978 was *Tradition Hall Jazz Band* on Sandcastle Records.

The band stayed busy with its regular jobs at Tradition Hall and Preservation Hall and spot jobs all over the city for society events and private parties. Bob, who had never quit his day job as a guard at the Orleans Parish House of Detention, switched to working from 1:00 a.m. to 9:00 a.m. at the coroners office. He'd finish playing with the band at midnight, pick up his cymbals and drive to his office, where he'd put a pillow on the floor, put the phone next to it and then lay down and go to sleep. If the phone rang at all, his job was to answer it and write up the paperwork that would accompany the arriving body. There was an on-call driver assigned to his office for morgue pick-ups throughout the night. Bob never once went into the morgue because, as he said, "There was nothing there for me. No reason to be there."

One night, when his driver was out on a call, a father and son came in to get a copy of the paperwork for a brother that had been killed. Bob was writing the report, but it was a busy night and he had to continue answering the phone. The men complained that he wasn't writing fast enough and then snarled that they were going to come back behind the desk and speed him up. Bob told them, "Come on," as he pulled a gun from the drawer.

Bob said, "The guys started talking shit at me. I picked up the phone and told dispatch I was having a problem and to send me a unit right away. I didn't want to get in a fight and mess up my hands."

The band made frequent trips to Europe, where it continues to have a staunch following. Belgium, Ireland, England and Germany always gave the band members a warm welcome, but Bob felt that the trip to Paris in 1995, when they played for the president of France, was the most hospitable. The rooms were private and in the best hotels. Paris and New Orleans have much in common, including a shared heritage of excellent food. Being from New Orleans, that was a big consideration.

Bob French, while touring France in March 1972. *Courtesy of the French Family Archive.*

Bob's son, Robert Jr., was stationed with the military in Germany and was able to drive to Paris to watch his dad and the band. Then the two men drove back to Germany for a short stay. As Robert Jr. tells the story, Bob had fallen asleep in the passenger's seat and woke up as Robert was driving on the Autobahn. Bob looked over at the speedometer and said to Robert, "Don't you think ninety-five is a little fast?" Before Robert could say anything, three cars in quick succession zipped past their car as if it were standing still. Bob said, "Never mind," and went back to sleep.

In 1999, the band was hired to play at the inauguration of the first democratically elected prime minister of Dominica. He had been in the audience at Donna's Bar and Grill, at 800 North Rampart Street, one Monday night and had fallen in love with the vocalist. He was trying to convince her to leave New Orleans, so he hired the band to have another chance to plead his case. The band that went to Dominica was composed

In Dominica, 1999. Todd Duke (g), Davell Crawford (p), George French (b), Sista Teedy Boutté (voc), Bob French (d), Leon "Kid Chocolate" Brown (tp) and Steve Walker (tb). *Courtesy of the French Family Archive.*

of Leon "Kid Chocolate" Brown (tp), Steve Walker (tb), George French (b), Todd Duke (g), Davell Crawford (p), Bob French (d) and Tricia "Sista Teedy" Boutté (voc). Kelly Love accompanied the group as the sound technician. The entire band returned to the United States, and in an unfortunate turn of events, the prime minister passed from a heart attack within three months.

In that same year, Bob French and Joris De Cock, from Belguim, co-produced *"10 jaar't Dreupelkot"* by Bob French's Original Tuxedo Jazz Band and Joris De Cock.

In 2000, Bob French's Original Tuxedo Jazz Band was playing a regular Monday night gig at Donna's. The band included Tricia "Sista Teedy" Boutté (voc); "Big Fine" Ellen Smith (voc); Wendell Brunious (tp); Leon "Kid Chocolate" Brown (tp); Freddy Lonzo (tb); George French, Irving Charles, Richard Moten or Chris Severin (b); Bill Huntington (bj); and Bob French (d). The piano on the bandstand had a steady stream of players, including

Davell Crawford, David Torkanowsky, Paul Longsreth, Matt Lemmler, Mari Watanabe and Edward Frank, a one-handed piano player who sat in on occasion. Bob has said Ed could play with one hand more than some people could play with four.

Richard Moten tells of many conversations he had with Bob where he spoke about his desire to have each musician complement the other and the group. He says, "Bob was more interested in playing for the purpose of the music, for the feel of the music, and not so much about following the notes. When we were playing at Donna's and things weren't happening on the bandstand the way Bob wanted them to, he could point out who wasn't playing for the group like a symphony conductor."

The band's gig at Donna's was advertised as Bob French's Original Tuxedo Jazz Band and Friends. Those friends came from all parts of the world to sit in with the band. They might be people who had met Bob and the band on one of their European or Asian tours, or they might be someone from here in the United States that made the trip to New Orleans specifically to ask to play with the band. A person's age or gender didn't matter, just interest and ability. All you had to do was ask permission, as one of the younger members of the New Orleans jazz community found out.

Near the end of a set one Monday night, Irvin Mayfield, a young standout trumpet player, stepped onto the bandstand with his trumpet and started to play with the band. Bob ended the song a bit prematurely and told Irvin to get off his stage and stay off until he learned some manners. Bob said, "If James Rivers or Ellis Marsalis walked in, that's cool. These are the people I came up with, they're my equals. I've got grandchildren older than Mayfield."

Donna's, the home of the brass band, was a small joint where Monday-night patrons could pay a ten-dollar cover to listen to traditional jazz and between sets eat a plate of red beans and rice, the traditional New Orleans Monday-night dinner.

That tradition of red beans and rice on a Monday night in New Orleans can be traced back to the 1700s slave rebellion in Haiti and the long struggle between the white French planters and the enslaved and free people of color. Many blacks were able to flee by boat to the closest port, the Port of New Orleans. Beans, especially red beans, were a mainstay in their native diet, and as they relocated here in the New Orleans area as free people of color, they introduced their long, slow-simmering method of cooking red beans and rice to this population.

Dried beans require a lengthy time to cook, and the Monday ritual of laundry would keep the cookstove heating water all day. On Monday morning, the red beans, celery, green pepper, onion, garlic and seasonings were put in a pot of water with sausage or some ham left over from the Sunday dinner. The bean pot would be able to simmer slowly, off to the side on the stovetop, until it was time for the evening meal.

The other venue in town where the band played on a regular weekly basis was the Fairmont Hotel. Albert French and the Original Tuxedo Jazz Band had a regular gig there for years before he left because of differences with management. In 2000, Bob French's Original Tuxedo Jazz Band was back at the Fairmont playing in the Sazerac Lounge with a five-piece band that accompanied Tricia "Sista Teedy" Boutté. His usual lineup was Wendel Brunious (tp), Freddy Lonzo (tb), Chris Severin (b) and Larry Sieberth (p), with Bob leading from his seat at the drums. Bob says, "At the Fairmont, I never had to ask for a raise. They'd just ask the bartender who was making the most money for the bar, and the next week we'd have a bigger paycheck."

Both albums—*Livin' the Legacy*, released in 2000, and *The Legacy Lives On*, released in 2001—were recorded in 2000 by Bob French's Original Tuxedo Jazz Band and Friends for Royal Tuxedo Records.

Cracker Barrel Old Country Store, with assistance from the National Council for the Traditional Arts, produced the Heritage Series of recordings, and in 2002, it released a compilation CD of Bob French's Original Tuxedo Jazz Band. On the back of the CD cover was the following quote: "Founded in 1910 by 'Papa' Celestin, the Original Tuxedo Jazz Band has the longest history of continuous performance in New Orleans. The last 25 years of its nearly 100-year history have been under the brilliant direction of Bob French, carrying forward the raucous, irresistible sounds of classic New Orleans jazz."

In 2003, Bob French's Original Tuxedo Jazz Band released *Three Generations* on Tuxedo Records, and in 2004, Bob had the band's Jazz Fest performance recorded for an album entitled *Live at New Orleans Jazz Fest 2004*.

The nineteenth-annual JazzAscona New Orleans and Classics Festival was June 24 through July 5, 2004, and Bob and the band were there. The festival had been started in Lugano in 1975 to showcase the music of New Orleans, though it took until 1983 for the first actual New Orleans musician, Thomas "Kid" Valentine, to be hired to play. By 2004, the festival was enjoying a location at the foot of the Alps next to the Lake Maggiore.

The musicians on that trip were Bob French (d), Wendell Brunious (tp), Troy "Trombone Shorty" Andrews (tp, tb), Stephen Walker (tb), Clarence Johnson III (sax), David Torkanowsky (p), Paul Longstreth (p), Chris Severin (b), Mitchell Player (b) and Ellen Smith (voc).

New Orleans has national parks unlike any other in the country. The hiking trails are city sidewalks, and the park rangers are musicians. The National Parks Service has a building in Armstrong Park, where there are exhibits surrounding the performance area that is used to present concerts by local jazz bands. The New Orleans Jazz National Park is in the old U.S. Mint Building at the foot of Esplanade within the confines of the French Quarter, just a few hundred feet from the Mississippi River. The park rangers showcase the music from New Orleans with daily living history concerts for groups of park visitors. The park's previous building was closer to the river, with a smaller stage and seating for maybe 150. The Tuxedo Band was hired every year for one of the daily living history concerts, and in 2005, they performed on May 7. The band that day was Wendell Brunious (tp), Fred Lonzo (tb), Clarence Johnson III (sax), Matt Lemmler (p), Bob French (d) and Tricia "Sista Teedy" Boutté (voc).

Chapter 22

Adjusting after Hurricane Katrina

B y mid-August 2005, Bob had the band playing a regular Monday night gig at Donna's, Friday and Saturday nights at the Fairmont and filling in with private parties and public events all over the city. In late August, however, the world watched as Hurricane Katrina devastated the Gulf Coast. In the aftermath of the storm, the manmade levees protecting New Orleans gave way, and 80 percent of the city flooded.

When New Orleans was reopened to residents in late 2005, Bob, who had evacuated to the Washington, D.C. area, was one of the first people to return. He found a place to stay, rented a car and started trying to find other musicians. The back of Bob's datebook from this time period has musicians names matched to an assortment of out-of-town addresses with the area codes for their phone access rarely shown as 504, the New Orleans area code. Few of the old numbers worked, and just finding out who was around to sit in with the band was a challenge. Though some had stayed in the city and some had been evacuated around the country, the slow, steady stream of musicians began returning home.

Since the mid-1990s, Bob had programmed the Tuesday morning *Traditional Jazz Show* on WWOZ-FM, the world-renowned community-supported radio station in New Orleans that featured New Orleans music twenty-four hours a day, seven days a week. The physical station had been flooded, so every Tuesday morning, Bob would drive an hour and a half to the station's temporary studio in Baton Rouge with a canvas bag full of CDs from his personal collection to be on the air from 9:00 to 11:00 a.m. As the station added to its broadcasting hours, he added his Friday morning *French*

Cookin' Show to his schedule. He used a lot of his airtime to try to convince other musicians that they should return to New Orleans, his gravelly voice constantly urging them to come home. He slowed his appeals when he realized many had no place they could come home to.

The Fairmont Hotel's basement was the only level that had flooded, but the entire building had been severely looted. The interior destruction kept it from reopening, which eliminated the band's regular Friday and Saturday night gig. Bob pulled a band together with Chris Severin (b), Craig Klein (tb) and Detroit Brooks (bj, g). They started playing at Donna's on Monday nights, where Bob led from the drum seat wearing an extra-large, red T-shirt emblazoned with the words "Trailer Trash" to celebrate life in his FEMA trailer. He did take time to explain why he was wearing the shirt and what he thought of the response President Bush, Governor Blanco and Mayor Nagin had to the flood and its aftermath. It wasn't complimentary.

In November 2005, Bob and the band were hired to portray a displaced New Orleans band in an episode entitled "The Christmas Show" for the television series *Studio 60 on the Sunset Strip*. The episode had been created to show the plight of out-of-work New Orleans musicians after the flood. Bob wasn't new to filming; in early 2005, he had been in a Michael Murphy

Bob French, 2007 *Courtesy of the French Family Archive.*

146

documentary titled *Make It Funky*, which was filmed onsite in New Orleans. Working on *Studio 60 on the Sunset Strip* required them to fly to California, and Bob returned from the trip with these three observations: "They put me behind a wall when we played so you can't see me. I get to keep the custom fit tuxedo and the red satin shirt that went with it. The food was awful, not a bowl of gumbo or red beans in sight."

In late June 2006, Bob and the band were back on the shores of Lake Maggiore in Switzerland for the twenty-first-annual JazzAscona Festival. Bob had pre-shipped a huge box of the band's CDs, which sold out almost instantly after their performance.

The next stop on the festival tour was the 2006 American Folk Festival held on the waterfront in Bangor, Maine, where another crate of CDs sold in a short time. Bob later remarked, "The people in Maine were so laid back and easy to get along with."

The band's portfolio at this time had a set list that included "Bill Bailey," "Satin Doll," "Do You Know What It Means to Miss New Orleans?," "The Second Line," "Darktown Strutters Ball," "Balling the Jack," "Hallelujah (I Love Him So)," "You've Got the Right Key, but the Wrong Keyhole," "Black and Blue," "A-Train," "St. James Infirmary," "Besame Mucho," "Just Squeeze Me," "Last Night on the Back Porch," "Don't Get Around Much Anymore," "At Last," "Muskrat Ramble," "Bourbon Street Parade" and "When It's Sleepy Time Down South."

In the summer of 2006, the band moved its Monday night gig to Frenchmen Street. It was at Ray's Boom Boom Room for a couple of years and then spent a short time across the street at Café Brazil before it settled in at the dba. The configuration of the band changed according to the night and could include, on trumpet, Leon "Kid Chocolate" Brown, Shamarr Allen or Troy "Trombone Shorty" Andrews. On trombone could be Steve Walker, Freddy Lonzo or Troy "Trombone Shorty" Andrews. On bass was George French, Chris Severin, David Pulphus or Richard Moten. On piano was David Torkanowsky, Mari Watanabe or Paul Longstreth, with Bob French on drums and "Big Fine" Ellen Smith, Yolanda Windsay, Kimberly Longstreth, Juanita Brooks or Tricia "Sista Teedy" Boutté with vocals. Friends were still encouraged to sit in, and there were guests on most Monday nights. There was a lot of clean-up work going on in the city that brought a steady stream of volunteers from all over the world. The audience was always packed with a rich mix of people, both local and visitors, who loved the city and the music.

The night a lot of people looked forward to each year was when Bob would celebrate his December 27 birthday. In 2007, when Bob turned seventy, the celebration was on Saturday, December 29, at Ray's Boom Boom Room at 508 Frenchmen Street. The fliers on the poles and walls all over Frenchmen Street and the French Quarter announced, "Very Special Guests and Free Food." The twenty-dollar cover, double the usual, gave patrons access to the buffet, where they could sample Ray's jambalaya, smothered chicken or pork chops, steamed crab and red beans and rice. Bob himself cooked the gumbo.

Bob and the band started the night promptly at 9:00 p.m. "Big Fine" Ellen Smith was the vocalist with the regular band of Shamarr Allen (tp), Steve Walker (tb), David Pulphus (b), David Torkanowsky (p) and Bob (d). Detroit Brooks sat in on guitar. About halfway through his first bottle of Courvoisier, Bob had Herlin Riley take over on the drums so he could sit back and watch as Al "Carnival Time" Johnson, Topsy Chapman and her daughter, Yolanda Windsay, sang.

Juanita Brooks, Detroit's sister and one of Bob's dearest friends, stepped onto the stage and took everyone to church. Bob, starting on his second bottle of Courvoisier, got up on the stage with her, and they started dancing—or more truthfully, bumping and grinding—with Bob taking off his jacket and using it to scratch his back. Amid cheers for their performance, Bob wobbled his way back to his seat in front of the bandstand and proceeded to empty the tip jar, a handful at a time and with much bowing, at Juanita's feet.

THE LADIES IN RED honored Bob French at their annual dinner on May 18, 2007. Bob's bio in their program read, "His musical skills have been appreciated by enthusiastic jazz audiences in Switzerland, Germany, England, Belgium, the Netherlands and France. Legendary musical artists such as Sugar Boy Crawford, Frog Man Henry, Dave Bartholomew and Earl King will attest to the musical talents of Bob French, who merely wants to continue the tradition of New Orleans jazz in his own way." The picture chosen to accompany his bio was Bob's picture from the cover of the September 2006 *Downbeat* magazine, which celebrated the musical families and heritage of New Orleans.

The New Orleans American Federation of Musicians Local 174–496, which had a membership of 800 before Hurricane Katrina, was able to maintain a number of its members by offering them a reduced rate for the year immediately after the flood. The union was able to help its members, with many of them receiving up to a few thousand dollars in relief. In 2007, the membership was around 680, and there was a concerted effort throughout the city to bring more musicians home. Many of the regular venues for musical performance were lost to the floodwaters, eliminating jobs for returning musicians.

In a 2007 article for the New Orleans Labor Media Project, Bob, a life member of the Musicians Local 174-496 explained to Linda Rapka that he had "found union work in nightclubs has become more scarce in New Orleans since Katrina. All the good joints are taken over by people not from New Orleans. They came in, and they started looking for people non-union because they know they can pay them less money. So that makes it difficult."

In a 2009 interview with Geraldine Wyckoff, he clearly voiced his opinion on what he and many other musicians see as a failing. "It's time for the city of New Orleans and the state of Louisiana to get off their hands and start appreciating what they have in this city as far as the talent. The musicians don't get their fair share here."

In an effort to help the musicians find affordable housing in the city, Harry Connick Jr. and Branford Marsalis, two native New Orleanians with strong ties in the music community, devised a plan for the Musicians' Village. They envisioned an intentional neighborhood where musicians could find inexpensive housing among like-minded professionals. With the help of Habitat for Humanity and generous donations from around the world, they have been able to purchase blocks of flood-ruined homes, remove tons of debris and arrange for the building of seventy-two New Orleans–style single and double residences in the Ninth Ward. Bob received one of these residences on April 14, 2007, when Jim Pate, executive director of the New Orleans Area Habitat for Humanity, presented Bob with a loaf of bread, a bottle of wine and the keys to his new home at 1741 Bartholomew Street.

Bob, a longtime mentor of both Harry Connick Jr. and Branford Marsalis, was quick to offer any help he could, knowing that the Musicians' Village would help get the city's music scene back to a healthy place. Whenever there was a public function to announce a step forward or a completed portion of the overall project, Bob and the Original Tuxedo Jazz Band were called on to play. He also became the unofficial tour guide for the village. He was able to intelligently answer questions and talk with authority about how the Ninth Ward looked before and after the flood and how much progress was being made.

When *This Old House* came to New Orleans to renovate and rebuild a house on the other side of Claiborne Avenue in the Holy Cross neighborhood, the show's producer did a turn through the Musicians' Village, where the show shot a segment from Bob's porch. Of course, music was involved, and Bob invited Clarence Johnson III over with his saxophone for some informal jamming.

Jazz Fest. Bob French (d), Branford Marsalis (cl), Bill Huntington (g), Shamarr Allen (tp), Troy "Trombone Shorty" Andrews (tb) and Leon "Kid Chocolate" Brown (tp). *Courtesy of the French Family Archive.*

The band played the New Orleans Jazz and Heritage Festival again in 2007, and during the festival, Rounder Records released a new CD in the Marsalis Music Honors Series entitled, *Marsalis Music Honors Bob French.* In June of that same year, the Original Tuxedo Jazz Band played the annual Seafood Festival in the French Quarter. Shamarr Allen (tp), Steve Walker (tb), David Pulphus (b), Mari Watanabe (p) and Bob French (d) backed up vocalist Ellen Smith.

Kermit Ruffins opened a club at 1200 St. Bernard Avenue in what had been Sidney's Saloon, which featured a slightly divided long room with the bar at one end and a raised place for the band at the other. The band played a regular Wednesday night gig there for a short while. For a cover of five dollars, you could listen to live local music while you enjoyed a plate of whatever Kermit, the king of barbeque, was cooking that night in the kitchen or in the portable barbeque smoker he kept in his truck bed.

In April 2009, Bob French's Original Tuxedo Jazz Band was back on Bourbon Street as the regular Monday night performers in Irvin Mayfield's

More than a Century of a New Orleans Icon

Jazz Playhouse at the Royal Sonesta Hotel at 300 Bourbon Street. The band had been bouncing from one small club to another trying to maintain a weekly following in venues where drinks were served in the traditional New Orleans plastic go-cup and there were more places to stand than sit. At the Jazz Playhouse, however, the decorating was traditional floor-to-ceiling draperies in a deep burgundy with gold accents against the background of dark wood and smoked-glass windows. Drinks were served in sparkling glasses by a spotlessly attired waitstaff. Seating was upholstered parsons and club chairs clustered in groups of three and four around small, round glass-topped tables, each with a glowing candle in a short, pierced metal holder.

The carpeted bandstand, two steps higher than the floor, appeared small at first glance. The piano was positioned to the far left of the stage, with the back legs of the wooden piano bench inches from the edge of the platform. Front and center on a small glass-topped table were orderly six- to eight-inch stacks of CDs, each stack containing a different title. The microphone stood in the apex of the curving front edge of the stage, easily accessible to the vocalist and the horn players who formed the front line. The far right of the stage had an intimidating array of drums and cymbals crowding a black leather stool that brushed the back wall. A separate microphone was positioned next to the drummer.

In an interview with Keith Marszalek, Bob said, "It's great to be back on Bourbon Street at a world-class hotel like the Royal Sonesta. The jazz tradition is critical to the future of New Orleans culture."

The musicians who made up the Original Tuxedo Jazz Band in the first weeks of that regular gig were Andrew Baham (tp), Fredrick "Freddy the Voice" Lonzo (tb), Mitchell Player (b), Paul Longstreth (p), Bob French (d) and Yolanda Windsay (voc).

Bob French explained:

I always try to hire good musicians. Why would I want to have a ragtag musician on my gig? Erving Charles was my main bass player till he died in 2003. Never had an argument with Erving, he was an excellent bass player and singer. He was always dressed correctly and on time. He kept a cigarette on the bandstand at all times. Stuck it in between the strings of the bass and would smoke nonstop. He was a comedian on and off stage. Chris Severin was an irregular member of the band since the '80s. Chris, at fifteen years old, went to Houston with Ellis Marsalis and me to play a gig. He was a monster bass player then and still is. David Pulphus, another bass player, is from St. Louis, wants the wrong football team to win and is a computer genius. Richard Moten has been with me since the days at Donna's. I want him to play with us forever. David Torkanowsky has been coming to my house since he's ten years old. David lived right by Tulane University, and we didn't live too far from Tulane. He used to come and hang around us when he was young. Used to call my mama "Mama Claudia." I'll tell you one thing about David. If you're right with him you can call him up, say, "I need a PA system, I need a piano," and he'll bring it to your house by himself. He's just like that. Crazy as a betsy bug, but he's a good kid.

The society gigs that had kept the band busy since Celestin's time continued, with the band still very popular for cocktail parties and weddings. In addition to the regular Monday-night spot at the Royal Sonesta, Bob kept the band booked for numerous private functions, public concerts and appearances, both locally and globally.

One of the few events that interrupted Bob's schedule was the yearly WWOZ Piano Night, which falls on the Monday between the two Jazz Fest weekends. This was started as a benefit to pay for a statue of Professor Longhair but has since become a benefit for the local radio station, WWOZ-FM. Bob, a longtime programmer for the station, had been a frequent master of ceremonies for the event. While he was entertaining the audience over at the House of Blues, the rest of his band, with a fill-in drummer, would be at their regular Monday night gig.

In June 2009, the band traveled to Washington, D.C., to perform at the Fifth Annual Duke Ellington Jazz Festival. Shamarr Allen (tp), Calvin Johnson Jr. (sax), Lucien Barbarin (tb), Bob French (d), Juanita Brooks and Al "Carnival Time" Johnson (voc) played on the stage designated "New Orleans on the Potomac" on Friday, June 12. On Saturday, June 13, the group played for the festival audience from the Kennedy Center's Millennium Stage.

In July 2009, "Kid" Merv (tp), Glen David Andrews (tb), Richard Moten (b), Paul Longstreth (p), Yolanda Windsay (voc) and Bob French (d) performed in Butte, Montana, at the seventy-first National Folk Festival. In the promotional material sent out by the National Folk Festival, it mentions Bob's dedication to jazz and his love of his city, New Orleans. "Bob French's Original Tuxedo Jazz Band has performed for presidents and kings and traveled the world. An icon in a city steeped in musical tradition, the group has become something more than just a band; it's an institution."

In October, the band flew to Richmond, Virginia, to perform for the Richmond Folk Festival, a successful offshoot of the National Folk Festival, which has been held in twenty-eight communities around the country and had been on Richmond's downtown waterfront between 2005 and 2007. The band included Andrew Baham (tp), Steve Walker (tb), Matt Lemmler (p), Danon Smith (voc), Richard Moten (b) and Bob French (d).

Chapter 23

The Centennial Year

2010

O n February 21, 2010, Bob French, Calvin Johnson Jr., Shamarr Allen, Lucien Barbarin, Al "Carnival Time" Johnson and Grammy-winning composer and singer Harry Connick Jr. went to the White House by invitation of President Barack Obama and First Lady Michelle Obama. On Sunday afternoon, the band performed for Mrs. Obama and members of a Washington elementary school glee club. The message to the children was that music can get people through the darkest times, even a disaster like Hurricane Katrina.

The men had the late afternoon to themselves and then returned to the White House at 7:00 p.m., when they were scheduled to meet President and Mrs. Obama in a private reception.

We were treated well. The Secret Service, they never smile, except for the cats in the door. They search you, every time you come in—worse than the airport. They ask us not to take any pictures, but you would know it and I would know it there would always be one jackass in the bunch. He had a good camera. I said, "Didn't the folks ask you, didn't they tell you not to? You know, man, you could get all of us shot. You know what the Secret Service is about. I mean, they leave their feelings out at the door." And I said, "There are rules, and rules are not made to be broken." But this boy's got about as much sense as a cockroach. So you know what I did? If he was over here, I got over there. They shoot the son-of-a-bitch, they won't shoot Bob. You know, I mean, you out there and you tell him not to use a camera and all of a sudden you see a flash and someone comes up with one of them guns and blow his ass away and I'm standing next to him. Just be my luck to get blown away too. So he didn't understand. He didn't want to understand. I learned a lot by being out here since I'm fifteen years old. I don't want to be anywhere where there's trouble. If trouble is to my right, I'm going to the left. I won't be no hero.

When the president and first lady arrived, there were no incidents, and Bob was impressed by the first couple for being so down-to-earth and easy to speak with. He said, "I felt very honored to be able to meet the first black man elected president of the United States, something I hadn't thought would happen in my lifetime. And Mrs. Obama…she's hot!"

Later that evening, the band played in the East Room for the president, the first lady and the members of the National Governors Association at the Governors' Ball, a black-tie event.

AT THE OPENING DAY of the New Orleans Jazz and Heritage Festival on Friday, April 23, 2010, Bob French and the Original Tuxedo Jazz Band's 100 Year Celebration had the 7:00 p.m. time slot to close out the Economy Hall Tent. The band has played Jazz Fest every year, including the early years, starting in 1948, when it was produced by the New Orleans Jazz Club. Bob had his cousin, trumpeter Dave Bartholomew, who was recently inducted into the Rock and Roll Hall of Fame, as a special guest. The tent was packed to overflowing, with many standing three deep at all the entrances. When the band played "The Saints," a spontaneous hip-shaking, umbrella-thrusting, dancing second line circled the entire seating area.

The performance was recorded and released as a CD courtesy of the New Orleans Jazz and Heritage Festival, WWOZ, 90.7FM and Threadhead Records.

On April 26, the Monday between the two Jazz Fest weekends, the Historic New Orleans Collection and Irvin Mayfield's Jazz Playhouse at the Royal Sonesta Hotel presented an evening of conversation and music to honor Bob French and the Original Tuxedo Band on their one hundredth anniversary.

The Historic New Orleans Collection hosted the first part of the evening in its Royal Street conference room. Robert Markham of the New Orleans Jazz Orchestra introduced Dr. Bruce Boyd Raeburn, head archivist at the Hogan Jazz Archives, and Bob French to the audience and then sat back as Bob, with Bruce's prompting, spoke about the history of the band.

Then it was on to Irvin Mayfield's Jazz Playhouse at the Royal Sonesta for four hours of traditional jazz as played by Bob French's Original Tuxedo Jazz Band.

The audience was celebrating one hundred years of history, but for the band, it was business as usual. Bob, wearing a dark purple suit, stood at the end of the bar talking with whomever was around. Hanging on the wall just over his shoulder was an oversized picture of Irvin Mayfield holding his trumpet and smiling down on the customers who were lining the bar. Bob whistled his trademark "call to post," a distinctive Eb-Bb-Eb-Bb bird-like warble, and then with an amber glass of Courvoisier in his hand, he walked toward the stand. By the time he was seated and everything within his reach was adjusted, the other dark-suited men—Andrew Baham (tp), Steve Walker (tb), Larry Sieberth (p) and Richard Moten (b)—had made their way to their positions. Though they were exchanging easygoing banter, they were ready to start.

Vocalist Yolanda Windsay—wearing a shimmering red jacket over a long black skirt, a sparkling tennis bracelet and earrings that almost brushed her shoulders—nodded to each of the men, disengaged the microphone from the stand, called the number and counted off the beat. With eyes closed and soft, open-palmed pats on her thigh to keep time, she waited to address the song.

The first three tunes were "Darktown Strutters Ball," "What a Wonderful World" and "Green Dolphin Street." Next, Bob called for, "You Are My

Centennial year, 2010. Andrew Baham (tp), Richard Moten (b), Yolanda Windsay (voc), Bob French (d) and Freddy Lonzo (tp). *Courtesy of the French Family Archive.*

Sunshine," which he turned into a singalong, yodels included. After the applause, Bob invited Mr. Meich, a German visitor, to sit in with his trumpet. His jeans and soft plaid shirt were a contrast to the dark suits of the rest of the men. Mr. Meich chose "Strutting with Some Barbeque" and took the first solo followed by Walker, Baham, Sieberth and then Moten.

Throughout the night, the men stood quietly when they weren't playing. They were respectful of one another and gave each soloist his space. Baham moved to the side of the piano and rested against it, leaning on his right elbow with his left hand holding the downward-pointing trumpet at ease at his side. His knees bent to allow his foot to keep time, never stopping. Walker, the trombone player, tried to stay out of the line of vision of the audience. With one foot on the stage and another one step down, he fixed his eyes on the bass player as he took his solo. Moten, at the end of his solo, gave a soft smile of acknowledgement to the applause.

Bob called to "take a little pause for a worthy cause" to the tune of "C-Jam Blues," the men put down their instruments, the house music came up and, one by one, the musicians left the stage. A white-haired man wearing deck shoes, well-pressed shorts and a pale blue camp shirt purchased a CD, shook Andrew's hand and then engaged Bob in a short exchange before Bob continued over to hug a woman who had requested a song earlier. A man passed by Yolanda and, referring to "What a Wonderful World," told her, "I danced with my daughter to that song at her wedding."

The rest of the musicians walked around greeting and talking with regulars and visitors alike for about twenty minutes before they congregated near Irvin's picture to order drinks. Bob whistled, and the second set was on.

The set list included "Amazing Grace," with Yolanda singing and Sieberth taking a solo; "Ain't Misbehaving"; "It Don't Mean a Thing If It Ain't Got That Swing"; "My Funny Valentine," which Bob dedicated to all the ladies in the house; and "Route 66." Then, as Moten played a solo on the bass, Bob introduced the band.

After another short break, the band was back for the final set, which included "Hello Dolly"; "I Left My Heart in San Francisco"; "Summertime," performed to a fast, swinging beat, as requested by Yolanda; and "In a Mellow Tone." At midnight, Bob closed out the evening with his trademark declaration, "If you liked the music, tell all your friends. If you didn't like it, don't tell nobody."

One year later, on May 2, the Monday between Jazz Fest weekends in 2011, Bob and the band were celebrating the start of their third year at the Royal Sonesta. Andrew Baham (tp), Steve Walker (tb), Richard Moten (b),

Larry Sieberth (p), Bob French (d) and Yolanda Windsay (voc) were playing to a packed house. Bob counted off the beat, and the band started "Sunny Side Of The Street." After a few measures, he pulled the low mike closer to his face and, in his pleasant but gravelly voice, welcomed everyone to the club and reminded them, to the expected laughter, that any request should be written on a one-hundred-dollar bill. The band moved into "The St. Louis Blues" and then "Night in Tunisia." Bob maintained a rock-steady beat with his distinctive New Orleans style of traditional jazz drumming. His gaze moved constantly from the bar to the door to whomever was moving around through the tables.

At a table near the bar, there were intermittent bursts of loud talking, and it was annoying Bob and the rest of the audience, so the next song he jokingly called for was "Silent Night," which got a laugh from the majority of the audience. Then he called Yolanda to the stage for "Basin Street Blues," "Since I Fell For You" and "When You're Smiling." As they went to break, Bob reminded everyone that the band was starting on their second century. "Just look at us!"

The second set included "After You're Gone," with Dr. David Blask from Tulane University sitting in with his trumpet; "St. James Infirmary" by request, with Andrew Baham on vocals; "Georgia On My Mind" by request, with Yolanda on vocals; "Summertime," which brought at least a dozen smiling couples to the dance floor; and "Do You Know What it Means to Miss New Orleans," with Kaleb Windsay, Yolanda's son, sitting in on trombone while Yolanda was on vocals.

The third set included "Do What You Wanna," featuring both Steve Walker and Kaleb Windsay on trombones with audience participation; "The Birth of the Blues," with guest vocals by Pippa Wilson from Melbourne, Australia; and "At Last," "Route 66" and "Fever," all featuring Yolanda on vocals.

The fourth set started with Bob singing "You Are My Sunshine," with enthusiastic audience participation and Bob's yodeling at the end. Irvin Mayfield sent up a dollar and requested "The Saints" as a joke. For years, the bands in town have posted signs that read, "Requests: Traditional songs—$1.00, "The Saints"—$5.00." The band played it after some good-natured ribbing back and forth between Bob and Irvin. Then "Happy Birthday" was sent out to James and Kaitlin, in the audience, as Bob continued to harass Mayfield. The final song for the night was one that "Papa" Celestin and "Papa" French had often used to close out their performances: "Goodnight Sweetheart," with Andrew Baham joining Yolanda for a duet.

Closing out at Jazz Fest has always been considered an honor. Bob and the band were back to play the final set, from 6:00 to 7:00 p.m., in Economy Hall on Sunday, May 8, 2011. The Neville Brothers had the same time slot on the Acura Stage, and the Radiators, who were dissolving as a band, were performing for the last time in public over on the Gentilly Stage.

The crowd in the Economy Hall tent was small at 5:45 p.m. when the band ran through the sound check. The musicians for the performance were Andrew Baham (tp), Steve Walker (tb), Don Vappie (bj, g), Richard Moten (b), Larry Sieberth (p), Paul Longstreth (p), Bob French (d) and Yolanda Windsay (voc). Bob had accidentally hired two piano players, and when they both showed up, he had to sort out who would play when. Moments before the 6:00 p.m. start time, Bob was at the edge of the stage in an argument with festival management as he insisted he had been told he could sell his own CDs privately from the stage, which is contrary to the festival's rules.

To the strains of "Sleepy Time Down South," Bob welcomed everyone to the performance and introduced the band. He then led them into "Sweet Georgia Brown," with solos that went from Walker to Baham to Sieberth and finally to a great slap solo by Moten. Next was, by request, "Basin Street Blues," with Vappie covering the vocals, and then "Muskrat Ramble," with Longstreth on the piano and Bob with the vocals.

At the end of the song, there was a slight pause in the music while Bob accused an unidentified person in the audience of video taping and demanded to have security remove the person and confiscate the camera. He pointed to the spot of the violation; a guard was sent but was unable to find anyone with a camera. All the while, Bob kept yelling, "Where you from?"

After the disturbance, the band came back with "Somebody Exactly Like You," with Don Vappie on banjo and vocals, and then "I Wanna Be A Rug Cutter." Bob took a short break to promote his CD from the 2010 Jazz Fest, featuring his cousin Dave Bartholomew on trumpet, by encouraging everyone to attend the CD release party at the Louisiana Music Factory on Monday, May 9. He was addressing a much-diminished audience as many had left to catch one of the other two bands playing the last part of their last sets on the last day. The small dance floor off to the side of the stage was empty, and there were more vacant seats than occupied, but the audience was full of applause as Bob called Yolanda to the stage. She started her set with "Darktown Strutter's Ball," with

Jazz Fest, 2011. Larry Sieberth (p), Don Vappie (g), Yolanda Windsay (voc), Richard Moten (b), Andrew Baham (tp), Steve Walker (tb) and Bob French (d). *Courtesy of Yolanda Windsay.*

Vappie on guitar and Sieberth on piano. Next was "Sit Right Down and Write Myself a Letter" and then "My Funny Valentine," with Longstreth taking a turn at the piano and staying for "Route 66." The set finished with "Good Night Sweetheart" as Yolanda was joined by Baham and Vappie for some harmonizing. It was a quiet ending, without the joy of a second line.

OVER THE LATE SPRING and early summer of 2011, Bob booked the band for very few jobs other than the regular Monday night at Irvin's Playhouse. The band traveled in mid-March to Washington, D.C., to perform for an Honor Award event at the National Building Museum.

We were playing inside. You should have seen this place. It was so beautiful. It's one of those old halls that they did completely over. We played, like, the bandstand was on the floor and the people were out there. They're like twelve to fourteen hundred people and all they were doing was eating. And they told us to be here a certain time. We're going in there early enough so we could eat. There's no food for us. Go upstairs and I'll bring you food. Food never came. Are they going to bring us any goddamn food or what? You know, I could have eaten at the hotel. And the hotel wasn't that expensive. So everybody in the band got pissed, you know, so they finally, they, in there what they brought wasn't the kind of meal I expected. Not the food I saw out there.

By this time, Bob's health had become an issue, and the years of refusing to acknowledge or control his diabetes were taking a toll. All trips to doctors and hospitals ended with the same results, as Bob was determined to do exactly as he chose. He occasionally showed up late, breaking the rule about which he had been unbending through his career. His father, Albert, had told him to be strict about being punctual, saying, "If you are hired to play at 8:00, be on the bandstand at 8:00, even if the room is empty. Play a song, and then go sit at the bar and wait til there are customers. As long as you're on time, they have to pay you."

There was an incident one night at the Sonesta when Bob stopped the band mid-song and told an imaginary person in the audience, "I know this is Bourbon Street, but on my bandstand, you don't just pull out your trumpet and start to play without asking permission. So put your instrument back in the case and sit your ass down." As this was happening, the men on the stage stood at "musicians attention," arms hanging loosely at their sides holding their instruments, blank faces with eyes straight forward focusing toward the ceiling. No one had seen this rogue trumpet player or anything out of the ordinary.

A few weeks later, before the evening began, he startled the audience by relating in a soft, halting voice, "I just had a woman break into my house, just now before I came here. She woke me up from a nap and asked for money. I didn't know her, but I went to the kitchen and got her some gumbo I had cooked yesterday." Looking confused, he serenely passed this off, saying, "This is what happens here in New Orleans, you just never know what will happen. We take care of each other." Then he counted off the first song, and the rest of the set went normally.

On Monday, July 18, 2011, the Tuxedo Band at Irvin Mayfield's Playhouse in the Royal Sonesta Hotel consisted of David Blask (tp), Steve Walker (tb), Richard Moten (b), Larry Sieberth (p), Bob French (d) and Yolanda Windsay (voc). Bob was on time because his son Albert had driven hime and helped set up the drums. The men in the band, all friends, wanted to help Bob maintain his dignity and were careful to act as if nothing were unusual, though his every action and thought were wrapped in confusion. From his perch on the drum stool, Bob called for tunes and then, completely out of character, sang along, unaware of what he was doing. While he was unintentionally disrupting the performance with his offbeat, tuneless drone in the background, his drumming was unwavering and in perfect time.

Toward the middle of the evening, Bob perceived the votive candles on the cocktail tables to be lights from videotaping devices and was convinced that people were recording his band for their own financial gain. He became too agitated to continue. Yolanda's husband, Mike Windsay, a more than competent traditional jazz drummer, helped Bob leave the stage and then took over the drums and finished out the night.

It was Bob's last night on the bandstand as leader of the Original Tuxedo Jazz Band.

Chapter 24
Gerald "The Giant" French

O n Tuesday morning, July 19, 2011, Bob was in a doctor's office getting yet another medical examination while Fred Goodrich from Musician's Village, who was helping to coordinate Bob's health care, Bob's son Albert and the author were in the waiting room. At 9:00 a.m., Albert left the room to take an incoming call. He returned wearing a relieved smile and explained that Gerald French had just agreed to be the next leader of the Tuxedo Band, as his Uncle Bob had requested. He was ready to assume leadership of the band whenever he was needed. He told Albert to pull the paperwork together, and he would sign it. There would be a smooth transition to the new leader.

In the past few years, Bob had made it clear to family and

Gerald French. *Photographer Jerry Moran, Native Orleanian Fine Photography.*

a few close friends that he wanted Gerald, his brother George's son, to become the next leader of the band. Bob had always said the first time he heard Gerald playing the drums, he thought he was listening to himself. Gerald himself has said, "I learned how to sing by listening to my dad and how to play drums by watching and listening to Uncle Bob."

Gerald Penelton "The Giant" French was born in New Orleans, Louisiana, on May 9, 1970, to George and Casandra Thomas French. He started playing the drums at the age of five, about the same time that he started kindergarten at Our Lady of Lourdes School, where he studied through eighth grade. After two years at the Eleanor McMain Secondary School, he left to spend his last two years at Alcee Fortier High School, where he marched in the band. He started his teaching degree at Southern University in Baton Rouge, finished it at Delgado College in New Orleans and was immediately hired as the assistant bandleader at St. Mary's Academy in New Orleans.

I was teaching music during the daytime and playing gigs at night, until I got a call one day from Leroy Jones in 1994, and he's like, "Brother Giant, you want to go on the road?" and I'm like, "On the road? Where?" and he's like, "I got the opening spot for Harry [Connick Jr.]. *You want to go on the road?" Like, yeah, I'll go, why not. So it wind up being I just thought it was gonna be a summer gig. And when school got ready to start I went back home and quit my job, and I've been playing music full-time ever since. You know, what I was making in one week out on the road with Harry is what I was making teaching school for a whole month. And we were just the opening band, we weren't even the headliners. Leroy's band was the Leroy Jones Quintet, and we opened for Harry Connick Jr. I was making fifteen hundred dollars a week, just opening, and that's salary plus per diem, you know, so I'm gonna ride this gravy train until it runs out.*

I did that thing with Leroy for about nine months, close to a year, and had a nice little nest egg. So I came back home and started gigging it. 1994 was where I stopped having a day job, and all I did was music and I've been doing that ever since. I've been playing with Charmaine [Neville] *for thirteen years. It's been a blessing. It's been a great experience. I played with everybody, for Phillip Manuel, Dr. John, Harry Connick Jr., Leroy Jones, Dr. Michael White, Preservation Hall, Fritzel's All Star Jazz Band, Tom Fisher, Jon Cleary and the New Orleans All Stars. Some others, but I worked with mostly local bands, but I worked with a lot, you know, local stuff. Henry Butler, everything from modern jazz to traditional jazz to funk and blues and everything in between. They call me The Giant, cause, cause of my size and also cause of my sound. Fred Lonzo gave me that name, and it stuck. When Freddy gives you a name, you can't get away from it. The Giant, yeah, Freddy gave me that name before anybody else started calling me that.*

As Bob's health deteriorated, the band's schedule had been reduced to the Monday night gig at Mayfield's Jazz Playhouse in the Royal Sonesta Hotel. July 25, 2011, was Gerald's first night as the drummer and leader-elect of the Original Tuxedo Jazz Band. The band he led that night consisted of the musicians Bob had been working with in the recent past: Leon "Kid Chocolate" Brown (tp), Steve Walker (tb), Richard Moten (b), Larry Sieberth (p), Gerald French (d) and Yolanda Windsay (voc).

At the start of the first set, with the other musicians standing in place and ready to play, Gerald adjusted his position behind the drums, took hold of the microphone and announced to the full house, "Good evening. I am Gerald French, and we are the Original Tuxedo Jazz Band. We're going to start with 'Shake It Don't Break It,' which is also known as 'The Weary Blues.'" He followed that with "The Bogalusa Strut," featuring Leon "Kid Chocolate" Brown. Then he passed along the bit of information that "it was Bob who gave Kid Chocolate that name." Next was "Why Don't You Go Down to New Orleans," with Gerald on vocals and a mention afterward that it had been recorded by his grandfather Albert French. This was followed by "Basin Street Blues," "Louisiana" and "I'm Gonna Sit Right Down and Write Myself a Letter," each with Yolanda on vocals. "Georgia" and "Please Don't Talk About Me When I'm Gone" closed out the set.

While everyone took a break, the author sat with Moten and Windsay as Gerald explained his vision for the future of the band.

There's a lot of songs they've been kinda pushing aside, so if I do officially become the leader of the band, I want to go back to playing a lot of those older songs, you know, if I gotta make CDs or have rehearsals or whatever. We need to preserve this thing, you know, and play some of the repertoire, and like I say, there's a handful of tunes that I remember as a kid sitting there listening to my grandfather play. Nobody plays these songs any more, nobody.

There's a lot of songs like "Whenever You're Lonely Just Telephone Me," that one, there's "Poor Butterfly," there's "March of the Bobcats," ah, "Tishomingo Blues," oh, there's a lot of songs that nobody plays no more.

Richard Moten said, "There's a lot going on in that song." French continued:

Yeah, oh yeah. You gotta know the song, you know, and that's what I want to bring back. I don't want to be the leader just to say I'm the leader. I want to have a band that can play both the swing and the modern kind of stuff, you know, that will please a general population. But, I also want to be able to, if I'm put in the situation where we have to do a concert and all we play is traditional jazz, I want to be able to play two sets of nothing but traditional New Orleans music. And play it the way it's supposed to be played, and that's what I wanna do. If I'm not gonna do it right I don't want to do it at all.

Yeah, you know, for me I have an advantage because those tunes were osmosis to me. What I mean by that is that it was always around me, it wasn't something that I had to go and search for or something that I had to look for. It was there. I've been in Preservation Hall one night, and I was playing with Wendell, and Wendell was like, "Brother Giant, what you want to play?" I leaned over to him, and I called uh, I said, "Let's play 'March of the Bob Cats' or 'Maryland, My Maryland' or 'Bugle Boy March,' something like that's got some past." He said, "Man, we can't play that, man, the cats don't know them sections. We can't play that." I say, "Well, you call something else then."

That's the tunes my grandfather and them played. Yeah, so there's a lot of that stuff just's been pushed under the rug. Yeah, cats don't want to do no homework, you know, they don't want to investigate those songs and then really do them, you know. So that's my goal, to try and get things back, back to…so beautiful, beautiful. So, that's my perspective. What I want to do.

I have some ideas of what I want to do and how I want to do things. I mean, my grandfather had a seven-piece band. Eventually, I want to get back to that and to have a full band, a full traditional band, you know, three horns and my grandfather played banjo, and he had four rhythm and three horns, and sometimes he would have a guest singer. You know, Miss Blanche Thomas used to work with my grandfather. She used to work with him for years. And so whenever they would do things overseas or they would do tours, it would be an eight-piece band. That was in the regulations. I want to get back to that. I want to get back to doing things the way they should have been cause without the banjo, you know, that gives it the New Orleans flavor. That gives it the real New Orleans sound, you know. And the banjo player that I have in mind, well, a couple of them I have in mind, they play both the banjo and the guitar. So it'll be good. So on the swing stuff they can play the guitar and on the traditional stuff they can play banjo.

"The World is Waiting For the Sunrise." That's a blast from the past. Wow. David Douglas, he gets up there. He played with Fat's Domino for years. And the band that we go to Japan with was led at one time by John Brunious, which is Wendell Brunious' brother. So, to make a long story short, David was great, as long as he didn't have to play any number where he was featured. He would get nervous, and he just wouldn't do what he was supposed to do. He wouldn't go in the shed and really practice. So one day, we're in Japan, and John's like, "Man, if you could play this songm I'll give you $500 extra dollars." We were at the public hall and they sat there between the two sets. It was like four hours between shows. They sat there for four hours trying to get David to play "The World is Waiting For the Sunrise" on the banjo. Could not do it…It was hilarious.

Then a quick question and answer ensued between Yolanda, who had been with the band for years, and Gerald, leading the band for the first time.

G. Yeah, yeah. We get off at 1:00?
Y. What?
G. We get off at 1:00?
Y. 12:00.
G. Oh. 12:00?
Y. 8:00 to midnight.
G. Good.

The second set opened with "Strutting with Some Barbeque" and then "Muskrat Ramble," with French providing vocals and a drum solo. Someone in the audience requested "Happy Birthday" for Jay, John, Dave and Kristi. Kid Chocolate sang the basic lyrics, including, "How old are you? May the good Lord bless you," and then added his own wish for them: "I hope you get some." "St. James Infirmary," "Bourbon Street

Gerald French and the Original Tuxedo Jazz Band, 2013. *Left to right*: Andrew Baham, Richard Moten, Larry Sieberth, Gerald French and Lucien Barbarin. *Photographer Jerry Moran, Native Orleanian Fine Photography.*

Parade," "Honeysuckle Rose," "My Funny Valentine" and "Darktown Strutters Ball" closed the set.

On November 21, 2011, the musicians that played at Mayfield's Playhouse included Leroy Jones (tp), Lucien Barbarin (tb), Richard Moten (b), Larry Sieberth (p), Gerald French (d) and Yolanda Windsay (voc). Jones filled in for Andrew Baham, the regular trumpet player, who was on a tour with another band. This has become the standard lineup.

The first set started at 8:00 p.m., with "The Bogalusa Strut." Then Gerald introduced the next tune as "a Louis Armstrong classic, 'Struggling with Some Barbeque,' I mean 'Strutting.'"

"Needs more tenderizing," was Barbarin's quick retort.

Each musician took a solo, and by the time Barbarin finished his trombone solo, there were people crowding through the door from the lobby and looking in through the courtyard windows. Everywhere there were people moving to the rhythm of the music.

Leroy called "Basin Street Blues," after which Gerald invited a guest vocalist from New York City to the stage, who called for "The Birth of the Blues." The band's long tradition of including guests continues.

The rest of the set included "Fidgety Feet," which Gerald introduced as an "old traditional number from about 1917 and one of Lucien's favorites"; "L Is For The Way You Look At Me"; "Honeysuckle Rose"; "Do You Know What It Means to Miss New Orleans," with Barbarin using a red rubber plunger to make the trombone "talk"; and "Bourbon Street Parade." At the end of the set, Gerald introduced the band and then let everyone know there were two CDs for sale, one from 1978 and one from Jazz Fest 2010.

The second set started a little after 10:00 p.m., as Gerald introduced the band to a much smaller audience and then called for "Muskrat Ramble," which, he said, "was written by Kid Ory and was Bob French's theme." Next was "Weary Blues," also known as "Shakin' an' Breakin' It," then "A Town Called New Orleans" and "Lil' Liza Jane."

Gerald called Yolanda up to the stand to the accompaniment of "My Satin Doll," and the band finished the evening with Yolanda singing "All Of Me," "It Don't Mean A Thing," "My Funny Valentine" and "When My Dreamboat Comes Home," with Paul Longstreth sitting in on piano.

On Monday, December 6, 2011, with all the paperwork legally signed and filed, there was a public ceremony at Irvin Mayfield's Jazz Playhouse in the Royal Sonesta Hotel as the leadership of the Original Tuxedo Jazz Band passed from Bob French to Gerald French. By 6:45 p.m., there wasn't a seat left in the house and barely a place to stand. Local dignitaries from the musical and political worlds were there to speak or just to witness an event that celebrated the legacy and acknowledged the future of a band that has become an institution in a city that treasures its musical heritage.

Irvin Mayfield welcomed everyone and started the evening's celebration.

Tonight we're here to celebrate history unfolding in front of our eyes, which makes us all part of history tonight. We have a great privilege and honor here at the Jazz Playhouse in the Royal Sonesta Hotel to start our Mondays with one of the most significant jazz institutions in the world. It is the longest continuous jazz band in the world, and we're really proud to be able to support it and recognize it here right in its own hometown.

When I had a conversation with Bob French maybe about a year and a half ago, we were at the Historic New Orleans Collection, and one of the things I asked Bob, after the performance and after his talk was over, [was] "What's your succession plan? What would you do?" He said, "Well, you know, I think my nephew, Gerald, will hopefully be interested in taking on the thing. I don't know on the basis of money for him, but..."

So Gerald and I, we had a solid conversation about it. One thing I'd like to just recognize, you know, here at the Jazz Playhouse, we have seven nights of music, sometimes we have up to three bands a night. Fact, we are the largest employer of bands of jazz in the city of New Orleans. Although we are deposited right in the heart of the city of New Orleans in the French Quarter and in the heart of that on Bourbon Street, we maintain our investment to the local community because we recognize it's really the locals who are the soul of what it is that has made this city so great. I've always said the city of New Orleans is known for the holy trinity: architecture, food and music. But really, it's the people who have elevated that through the time and it's those people [the locals] are some of the greatest creative world in American genius around, and I really believe that the Original Tuxedo Jazz Band, starting off with Oscar Papa Celestin and to Papa French then to his son, Bob French, and now to his nephew, Gerald French, is an example of the type of legacy we have in New Orleans, which is really unparalleled by anyone in this type of music in the world. So we're really excited about tonight, you know, it's something we're gonna look back on and remember for the rest of our lives. And to give you a little bit more on that, my business partner here and a number one supporter of jazz and the hospitality industry, the general manager of the Royal Sonesta, Mr. Albert Gross.

Albert Gross took the stage.

First, let me acknowledge Jack Lawrence of the Historic New Orleans Collection, who has really helped us out with the centennial celebration about a year ago. Over a year ago, we're in 101 now. And we work with them all the time doing our historical research investigations all the time. This is a special night. One hundred and one years old. I remember when Irvin and I were opening this beautiful venue, we were talking about different things and Irvin was giving me ideas, and he said to me there's no question that Monday nights we need to get Bob French. And we talked about it, and so they've been here right from the very, very beginning at the Jazz Playhouse. Now, I know 3 years is not 101, it's not at all, but I can tell you that we at the Royal Sonesta, we are pleased as punch to be a small part in the rich history of this wonderful band and family and so glad that it's continuing on into the future and so, anyway, thank you very much.

Irvin Mayfield continued, "You know, in New Orleans, we love all our festivals, and we love our posters. So we need, right now, to present the family with a commemorative poster of Bob French's first night here at the Playhouse. We put a gold plaque on it 'cause we knew Bob wouldn't have it any other way."

At this, Gerald French interjected, "You got that right."

Irvin went on to introduce the next speaker, saying, "We'd also like to bring up our representative from the city of New Orleans. She has been representing this community and in our city for a very long time, also multi-generational as well. Not in music, but in politics. But also in a sense of being a great patron and supporter of the arts. My good friend Miss Jackie Clarkson."

Good evening. Thank you so much. On behalf of the city council, that I am honored to be president of, and on behalf of the mayor and the whole city, let me tell you what a privilege it is to be here tonight. Yes, I am a supporter of the arts...and especially jazz and especially music... All of my life, I grew up here, here in New Orleans. And thank you to the Royal Sonesta Hotel, one of my favorite hotels. And thank you, Mr. Irvin Mayfield, for bringing jazz back to Bourbon Street.

I was first coming to the French Quarter to jitterbug in the late '40s. I danced to the Original Tuxedo Jazz Band and am proud to say I'm that old and proud to say I can still jitterbug. Irvin has seen me do it on this stand. I was here when he opened this because I do like to celebrate any of our history in jazz. My two favorite things in this city are jazz and opera because it was the two original art forms of music, and we had the birth of jazz and the longest existing operating opera house in North America. How's that for a city? I was just with Gerald earlier today as he played with Michael White at Arthur Davis's memorial service, which was quite a tribute to an icon in this city, and celebrated with music. His son being the legendary founder of jazz fest, Quint Davis. And so we celebrate everything with music in this city. What an honor to be with Al Gross and the Royal Sonesta and with Irvin Mayfield. You know what Irvin Mayfield really is. He really is New Orleans' cultural ambassador. It's an honor to be here tonight presenting a proclamation to the Original Tuxedo Jazz Band. I get to present it to

Gerald French, but I danced with Bob French. It says: "Whereas the city of New Orleans is renowned for its food, festivals, famous citizens and foreign visitors, we take great pride in paying tribute to Bob French and the Original Tuxedo Jazz Orchestra. Be it proclaimed by the city of New Olreans that the council recognizes Bob French, 34 years of band leadership of the Original Tuxedo Jazz Band. Thank you for 101 years of continuous jazz, not just continuous but top jazz for the world from the city that created it." Thank you.

After Miss Jackie Clarkson spoke, Gerald French took the stage.

Thank you guys. Thank you. I want to thank everybody that came out, especially my mother. Those are my sisters and brothers. And also my wife, she's here. Today we recognize this is not only a historic moment in time, but as I said before, the band started in 1910, so I got some big shoes to fill. My direction is basically to go back to the roots when the band started, and for those of you who are going to stick around for the performance tonight, we're going to have an actual full band tonight. We'll have a banjo, clarinet, trumpet, trombone, bass, drums and piano. And this is the proper way that this music should be played. I watched the video from 1965 of the band live in Germany. There was a video recording. It was quite impressive to see my grandfather much younger than I remember him as a child. I was born in '70, and he died in '77, so we had seven years. Not only was he a good bandleader but also an awesome grandfather. I had two sets of grandparents that were tremendous: Albert "Papa" French and Claudia, [and] also George Thomas and Victoria Thomas. My mother's father was the treasurer of the original Olympia Social Aid and Pleasure Club. So I had the chance as a kid to get both sides of the New Orleans tradition. My father's father was a bandleader and carpenter and housepainter and played music at night. And my mother's father was a tailor during the day and was treasurer of the social aid and pleasure club in the evenings. And also was a Mason, so I got a chance to get a little insight on that too. So I got New Orleans culture from both sides. I got the street culture and also got more of the society culture 'cause my grandfather played for the Boston Club, New Orleans Country Club and these big organizations. So for me, like I said in the interview I did for Lagniappe, it's a bittersweet time. I'm very happy because I'm able to fit in these shoes, and I also am able to take the band in the direction I think it should be going. But I'm also kind of sad because of my uncle's ailments and what's going on with him. So I want to thank you guys for coming out and for those people who are going to stay. You're in for a real treat tonight, and we're going to have some fun. Thank you.

Irvin Mayfield continued:

Well said. The last part of the ceremony, before we cut this cake, is the passing of the drumsticks, won't take long. And now, something we never do in this kind of things: talk about the music. Therefore, there are not that many drummers in the city of New Orleans who know the old—we call it the old, but the real style. There are probably really about seven or eight, and you know some of them are moving up in age, and this is something we have to figure out as a city. How to continue. Unfortunately, I don't know who the next Gerald French is right now. I've been meaning to figure that out. It's really important. Hopefully he or she, whoever it may be, or it, you never know. What I will say that this is the real deal, and we at the Sonesta are here to make an investment, not because of the return we make financially only, but I made the investment because artistically, that's what it's about. And when Gerald and I sat down and when I'm with every musician. We make the largest investment out of the week on Mondays because of what the Original Tuxedo Jazz Band, because Bob French and Gerald French and Papa French and Oscar Papa Celestin have represented. And I am forever humble to continue to be able to make that investment 'cause this investment and this music is so much larger than the individual, and I think as a city, it's the music is what the magic is. If we can do what the music has done, we can go much further as a society, and the passing of these drumsticks is representative of the fact that we are all here for a temporary moment, but the great things in humanity, the things we call art, those things are here for the continuum of human existence. And after all, tonight is about the things that are greater than an individual. The greatness of we. And so I'd like to give Al Gross an opportunity to pass on, symbolically, the drumsticks from the legacy of the Original Tuxedo Jazz Band, now 101 years and running, to Gerald French.

As Al Gross handed over the drumsticks, Irvin continued. His name is on those drumsticks. This is the real deal. We even put a $100 *bill in there, once again, to celebrate Bob. OK, one Bob French story, and then we gonna cut the cake. So, Bob and I got off onto the wrong foot somewhere. I really can't remember the story. There are a million different stories of it. I swear to God, I can't remember which night it was, but I think what happened, if I can go back, I believe there was one night I happened to be at Donna's Bar and Grill, and I happened to walk up on stage as Bob was getting ready to end his set. And so I jumped up on stage and took a solo. Now, here's the thing, the thing that I think happened. I was actually invited up there by Leroy Jones. I believe that's what happened. This is what Leroy had told me. Leroy said, "Come on up and get up on stage." I got up, and I played, and when you know things about New Orleans, you definitely know when you might be a pawn in somebody else's experience. So those things, these things happen. I think Leroy threw me under the bus. I'm gonna blame the shit on Leroy now, cause Leroy's not here.*

Anyway, I got up, and I played, and Bob never addressed it with me personally, but he had a unique way of addressing things. Imma call it the New Orleans sophisticated subtle approach. He went on the radio the next day and say he was going to whip my ass. And so after reading several blogs and having several people say, "Bob French say he gonna whip your ass," I say, "Well, you know, I'm just going to chill it out." Bob and I had this thing running for however long. And then I heard Bob discussing on the radio. He say hotels used to be the place where all the great jazz guys played. He says there's a lack of hotels with jazz anymore. I happened to have a discussion about a month and a half later, and I heard what Bob was saying, and that's kinda where I got the idea and sat down with the accountant and I say make this long-term investment in a hotel where I came from. So actually it was kinda, sorta Bob French's idea. I couldn't say it before 'cause I would have had to pay him. Now that he's not here also I get to get away with that. Laurie Tenneyson worked for me, and we called Bob. Then I sat down and say OK, we have to have this discussion, now how to do it? Well, I called up my good friend Dion Brown, and I said, "What does Bob drink?" And he said, "Bloody Marys." So, I made sure I had like the best most alcohol feels Bloody Marys for Bob when we sat down. So Bob sat down and had one Bloody Mary, and I said, "Now, I think you should have just one more." So we sat and had the second one. By the time I knew he was, you know, just right, I gave him the idea and said, "Let's do this thing on Monday night." And Bob said, "OK, how much money we talking about?"

And so then Bob and I came together right where mostly Bob and friends come together, right at the price of cost for his service. We both agreed on that cost, and we been friends again ever since. So I would like to raise our glass here. Oh yeah, champagne. To Bob French, one of the greatest characters New Orleans has ever known. Now, the reason we are all here, thank you all very much one again to Gerald French and the Original Tuxedo Jazz Band. How about it!

Mayfield turned the evening over to Gerald, who welcomed everyone from his seat behind the drum set on the bandstand with the following:

We are the Original Tuxedo Jazz Band. Yes, indeed. Right now, I'd like to take this time to introduce you to the guys in the band, and this is where the pleasure as well as the pressure work.

First and foremost, on the piano. We like to call him the professor. Please give it up for Mr. Larry Sieberth. Yes, indeed.

On the banjo, y'all. My partner in crime. I know you good. We gonna let you stick with that story tonight. We were together the last four or five years with the Charmaine Neville Band and even before that all around town. I used to see him when I was a little boy. 'Scuse me. I'm sorry. I used to see him playing at various churches around town. Ladies and gentlemen, the incomparable Mr. Detroit Brooks. Or as we say, Albert Brooks. 'Scuse me, I'm sorry. Yes, indeed.

On the trumpet, he's a tuned-up man around here. Our resident sound person. I'm sorry, over here, our resident trumpeter, vocalist, also our sound man, please give it up for Mr. Andrew Baham. Dance instructor, choreographer, put that together. Wait til that beat. He got that old-school grand marshal moves.

On the bass, y'all. Sometime I can't play the drum, and I just have to look at him. We been all over the world together. Japan several times, and other places around the world and not only is he a great bass player, but he's one of the nicest people you'll ever meet in your life. Please give it up for Mr. Richard Moten.

Almost done, Lord have mercy. Yes, indeed. A la qua. Where you at Book? Yes indeed. Well, this introduction here goes back to the heyday of the Original Tuxedo Jazz Band. His uncle, Mr. Louis Barbarin, was a drummer for many, many years in this great band and also his uncle Paul Barbarin played with Louis Armstrong for many years. Please give it up for the one and only Mr. Lucien Barbarin. As Drew like to say, Uncle Lucien. Uncle Lucien. He's been upgraded, up the stairs, Uncle Lucien. All right. How do you sleep at night? I heard you.

Anyway, y'all, on the clarinet, we've been all over the world together. Japan. Switzerland. Been many places together, and we won't talk about some of the places. And we worked together every Tuesday and Wednesday night down the street. I'm not going to mention the name of the place, but we work together on Tuesdays and Thursdays. And also he leads the New Orleans All Stars. We went to Japan and not only a nice guy, but he's also our resident health critic, and he drinks apple juice, as you can see. Free range apples. Anyway, on the clarinet, y'all, my favorite, please give it up, y'all, for Mr. Tom Fisher.

Last, but not least, trouble, trouble, trouble. She always blames us for stuff. I don't know why, it's just how ladies do. Blame us for things we have no control over. She comes from a long line of talented and beautiful women and is also beautiful. Very talented and an asset to this band. Please y'all give it up for Miss Yolanda Windsay.

Allright, my name is Gerald French, and so we gonna get down to business. I got the whole band tonight. We gonna bring back some of that old-time religion. Hope you all ready for this. 'Cause this is the way the music is supposed to sound and the way the music should be played, and we gonna play some of the older numbers that a lot of the younger musicians don't play, and we gonna get started on that. I was about to have a Bob moment there. I try not to.

I also want to recognize my family who's in the house. Don't start no stuff, we got a lot of Frenchs in here. Might be some trouble, might be some trouble. First and foremost, I'd like to introduce my cousin Joycelyn, she's Bob's oldest daughter, and her husband, and Bob Jr. is around here somewhere. He's got ants in his pants and need to dance. But anyway, also want to recognize my mother who's sitting up front, also my sister Cassandra French, my wife, Tiffany, and the apple of my eye, she's sitting up front, my daughter, Kamilah.

So, we gonna have a good time tonight and looks like we have a captivated audience. We gonna get things started. We gonna go back to the year 1923. Anybody been around then? This was recorded by another New Orleans Band, the Sam Morgan Band. This has been a staple of the band's repertoire for many years. This is the Bogalusa Strut.

And so it continues. This band has been here in this city and played for this city for over a hundred years. The music is the same; only the players change. The leader is new but cut from the old cloth. The band plays a mix of songs, including some that Celestin blew back before this leader and these musicians were born. The feeling is the same. The magic is the same. In your heart, you know that when they celebrate two hundred years, this is how it will be.

Epilogue

Bob French passed early in the morning of November 12, 2012. A public visitation and musical tribute was at the D.W. Rhodes Chapel, at 3933 Washington Avenue, New Orleans, from 1:00 p.m. to 3:00 p.m. on Saturday, November 17. The service was well attended and old-school respectful, as Bob had been adamant that there be no modern second line parade with its carnival atmosphere.

Gerald and the Tuxedo Band, with Richard Moten, Larry Sieberth, Detroit Brooks, Tom Fischer, Wendell Brunious, Lucien Barbarin and Yolanda Windsay, were the backup band for a number of guest musicians who came to honor Bob.

Solid Harmony, the mother-daughter trio of Topsy Chapman, Jolynda Phillips and Yolanda Windsay, was perfect with "Highway to Heaven," followed by Andrew Baham, who called for "St. James Infirmary." After a short silence, Don Vappie pulled on his banjo and said, "I can hear Bob saying, 'Why didn't you have your banjo ready? Quit wasting time on my gig!'" He played and sang to "The World is Waiting for the Sunrise," "I Just Want to be a Rug Cutter" and "Down by the Riverside"—the Sam Morgan version, about which his ninety-three-year-old mom says, "This is how they played it when I was a girl." Halfway through the song, he said, "You all better start clapping before he wakes up and tells you about it." And when it was finished, his final remark was: "There was Baby Dodds, there was Barbarin, then there was Bob. He's in that line."

Yolanda came to the microphone next, and before she sang "My Funny Valentine," she said, "Uncle Bob made me sing this every week. He'd say, 'You know I want you to sing this song.'"

Celebrating the Life of New Orleans Music Legend

Robert "Bob" French, Sr.

Pallbearers

George French, Sr.	Robert French, Jr.
Albert French	Gerald French
Gerard French	David Torkanowsky
Paul Longstreth	

Robert "Bob" French, Sr.

INTERMENT—PRIVATE

December 27, 1937—November 12, 2012

In lieu of flowers, the family would like donations made to the Ellis Marsalis School of Music, 1901 Bartholomew St., NOLA 70117, checks make payable to NOHMV, for scholarships in memory of Robert "Bob" French Sr.

DW Rhodes Chapel

3933 Washington Ave. NOLA 70125

Saturday, November 17, 2012

Visitation and Musical Tribute

1:00 pm — 3:00 pm

Thank you to all of our family and friends who have assisted us during this difficult time.

Professional Services & Arrangements Entrusted to:

D.W. Rhodes Funeral Home

Layout & Design by: Rhodes Publishing

Program from the Visitation and Musical Tribute to Bob French on November 17, 2012. *Courtesy of the French Family Archive.*

Leroy Jones was called by Gerald to sing next, and as he took the microphone, he looked at Gerald and said, "Why I have to come up after Yolanda, I don't know." He called for "When It's Sleepytime Down South" and then "Bourbon Street Parade." Bob's cousin Raynetta Owens-Brown sang "Eye on the Sparrow," and then the band played "Panama," with solos all around.

Wendell Brunious called for "It Ain't What You Do (It's the Way That You Do It)" and added, "Bob had an answer for everything, but he loved me and I loved him."

Dave Bartholomew, Bob's cousin, stayed in his seat facing the band and spoke the words to "The Monkey Speaks His Mind" without musical accompaniment.

"I'll Fly Away," "The Saints" and "In the Sweet By and By" were the final three tunes and it was over.

Bob's ashes are with his son, Albert.

THE ELLIS MARSALIS CENTER for Music hosted an invitation-only tribute for Bob on Tuesday, December 4, 2012, from 4:00 p.m. to 6:00 p.m. Harry Connick Jr. and Branford Marsalis started the musical part of the program with "Just a Closer Walk" as a piano/saxophone duet. They were joined by George French (b), Gerald French (d) and Dr. John (g) for "They Don't Want to See Me with You." Over the course of the evening, Shamarr Allen (tp), Calvin Johnson (cl) and Steve Walker (tb) joined the band for a song or two. Al "Carnival Time" Johnson (voc, p) performed "Carnival Time," Ellen Smith (voc) sang "Do You Know What it Means to Miss New Orleans" and Silent Harmony, the mother/daughter trio of Topsy Chapman, Yolanda Windsay and Jolynda Phillips, (voc) performed "Basin Street Blues."

There was a proclamation sent by Mayor Mitch Landrieu, and Dwayne Breashers from WWOZ.FM spoke. Anne Marie Wilkins shared how she had called Bob in 2006 and told him a black man, with whom she had professional connections, was running for president and was going to win. Bob assured her, "That will never happen in my lifetime." She kept him up to date on Barack Obama's progress, constantly telling him how this man was going to win. The morning after the election, she got a call from Bob. He wanted to tell her how astonished and proud he was that what he had thought was inconceivable had happened. And he wanted her to get him an invitation to the White House to meet the new president. Nothing less would do.

When she called the White House, the Secret Service googled Bob and told her, "No way. Have you seen his profile?" Bob was typically outspoken, and this profile may have had information about things he had said about the government in the past. She persisted, promising to be personally responsible for his behavior and included Harry Connick Jr. in the deal. The Secret Service relented, with reservations, and the date was set.

Bob and the band flew to Washington, D.C., and performed in the afternoon for Mrs. Obama and the schoolchildren. They were back to the White House at 7:00 p.m. for their private audience with president and Mrs. Obama. Anne Marie had him in her sight the entire time, and everything had been going smoothly. She could see Bob's face as he conversed with the first lady. He was so focused he had no idea the president had entered the room and was approaching him from behind. She saw the president put his hand on Bob's shoulder and watched as Bob started to turn with his face registering a look that could only be interpreted as: Can't you see I'm talking to a beautiful woman and don't want to be disturbed? The Secret Service and Anne Marie were to his side in the split second it took for Bob's expression to change to admiration. The men shook hands as Bob said, "Mr. President, it's an honor to meet you."

Discography

Original Tuxedo Jazz Orchestra
Celestin (cnt), Madison (cnt), Ridgley (tb), Thoumy (cl), Manetta (p), J. Marrero (bj), S. Marrero (b), Foster (d, slide whistle).
Okeh Records
January 23, 1925
Original Tuxedo Rag, Careless Love, Black Rag, High Society.

Celestin's Original Jazz Orchestra
Celestin (cnt), Rousseau (tb), P. Barnes (cl, as), Earl Pierson (ts), J. Marrero (bj), Salvant (p), Foster (d), Gills (voc).
Columbia Records
April 13, 1926
I'm Satisfied You Love Me, My Josephine, Station Calls, Give Me Some More.

Celestin's Original Jazz Orchestra
Celestin (cnt), R. Alexis (cnt), Rousseau (tb), P. Barnes (cl, as), Earl Pierson (ts), Carriere (ss, ts), J. Marrero (bj), S. Marrero (b), Salvant (p), Foster (d, voc), Gills (voc), F. Joseph (voc).
Columbia Records
April 11, 1927
Dear Almanzoer, Papa's Got the Jim-Jams, As You Like It, Just For You Dear I'm Crying.

CELESTIN'S ORIGINAL TUXEDO JAZZ ORCHESTRA
Celestin (cnt), R. Alexis (cnt), McCullum (cnt), Rousseau (tb), W. Matthews
    (tb), C. Hall (cl, as), O. Alcorn (cl, ts), J. Marrero (bj), S. Marrero (tu),
    Salvant (p), Frazier (d), Alexander Sr. (arr).
Columbia Records
October 25, 1927
When I'm With You, It's Jam Up.

CELESTIN'S ORIGINAL TUXEDO JAZZ ORCHESTRA
Celestin (cnt), G. Kelly (cnt), E. Kelly (tb), Earl Pierson (cl, as), Carriere (cl,
    ts), N. Kimball (bj), S. Marrero (bb,tu), Salvant (p), Foster (d, voc).
Columbia Records
December 13, 1928
Sweetheart of T.K.O., Ta Ta Daddy.

CELESTIN'S ORIGINAL TUXEDO ORCHESTRA
Celestin (tp), W. Mathews (tb), Picou (cl), P. Barnes (as), Lee (ts), Verret (g), R.
    Alexis (b), M. Fields (p), Goldston (d).
Deluxe Records
October 26, 1947
Eh La Bas; Marie Laveau; My Josephine; Maryland, My Maryland.

"PAPA" CELESTIN AND HIS TUXEDO JAZZ BAND
Celestin (tp), W. Matthews (tb), Picou (cl), R. Alexis (b, voc), Crosby (p),
    Goldston (d).
New Orleans Bandwagon
1949 Broadcast
Lil' Liza Jane, My Josephine, 12th Street Rag, Basin Street Blues, Clarinet
    Marmalade, Marie Laveau, Who's Sorry Now, Tiger Rag, Saints.

February 15, 1950 Broadcast
Saints, Lil' Liza Jane, Didn't He Ramble, High Society.

April 22, 1950 Broadcast
Panama, Tiger Rag, Dippermouth Blues.

April 24, 1950 Broadcast
Marie Laveau.

April 29, 1950 Broadcast
Didn't He Ramble, High Society, Fidgety Feet.

May 6, 1950 Broadcast
Milneburg Joys; Maryland, My Maryland; Eh La Bas.

May 13, 1950 broadcast
Woodchoppers Ball, War Clouds (Fidgety Feet), Sweet Georgia Brown.

July 1, 1950 Broadcast
Jazz Me Blues, It Don't Mean a Thing.

July 8, 1950 Broadcast
Sister Kate, Ballin' the Jack, Lady Be Good.

July 22, 1050 Broadcast
Sheik of Araby, Lil' Liza Jane.

Summer 1950 Broadcast
Bill Bailey, Mama Don't Allow.

September 2, 1950 Broadcast
Panama, Muskrat Ramble.
With Leonard Mitchell (bj); Old Time Religion.

November 14, 1950 Broadcast
Tiger Rag.

1950–1951 Broadcast dates unknown
Intro; Marie Laveau; Old Man Mose; I Got Rhythm; Maryland, My
    Maryland; San; Jada; A Closer Walk With Thee; Didn't He Ramble;
    Nellie Grey; St. Louis Blues; Bill Bailey; Mama Don't Allow.
June 9, 1951 Broadcast
Darling Nellie Grey, Saints, St. Louis Blues.

OSCAR CELESTIN AND HIS TUXEDO JAZZ BAND
Celestin (tr), Pierson (tb), P. Barnes (cl), Verret (bj, g), Porter (b), M. Fields (p),
    Louis Barbarin (d).

July 28, 1951 Broadcast
Lil' Liza Jane, Darktown Strutters' Ball, Saints.

OSCAR CELESTIN AND HIS TUXEDO JAZZ BAND
Celestin (tr), Pierson (tb), P. Barnes (cl), Verret (bj, g), Porter (b), M. Fields (p), Louis Barbarin (d).
1951 Broadcast
Basin Street Blues, Didn't He Ramble, Nellie Grey, Darktown Strutters' Ball, Saints, Lil' Liza Jane, Basin Street Blues.

OSCAR CELESTIN AND HIS TUXEDO JAZZ BAND
Celestin (tr), Pierson (tb), P. Barnes (cl), Verret (bj, g), Porter (b), M. Fields (p), Louis Barbarin (d).
1951
Tiger Rag.

OSCAR CELESTIN AND HIS TUXEDO JAZZ BAND
Celestin (tr), Pierson (tb), P. Barnes (cl), Verret (bj, g), Porter (b), M. Fields (p), Louis Barbarin (d).
1950s
Muskrat Ramble, High Society.

OSCAR "PAPA" CELESTIN AND HIS NEW ORLEANS BAND
Celestin (tp), Pierson (tb), Thomas (cl), Alexander Jr. (as), A. French (bj), S. Brown (b), J. Kimball (p), Louis Barbarin (d).
Columbia Records
November 1953
Intro, Tiger Rag, Darktown Strutters' Ball.

OSCAR "PAPA" CELESTIN AND HIS NEW ORLEANS BAND: GOLDEN WEDDING
Celestin (tp), Pierson (tb), J. Thomas (cl), Alexander Jr. (as), A. French (bj, g), S. Brown (b), J. Kimball (p), Louis Barbarin (d).
Southland Records, Storyville Records
April 24, 1954
Do You Know What It Means to Miss New Orleans, Down by the Riverside, Saints, Didn't He Ramble, Marie Laveau.

EDDIE PIERSON'S BAND
Walters (tp), Pierson (tb), J.Thomas (cl), A. French (bj), S. Brown (b), J. Kimball (p), Louis Barbarin (d).
Good Time Jazz
March 17, 1956
Gettysburg March, Gloryland, Bill Bailey.

CELESTIN'S TUXEDO JAZZ BAND
Walters (tp), Pierson (tb), J. Thomas (cl), A. French (bj), S. Brown (b), J. Kimball (p), Louis Barbarin (d).
Jazz Crusade Label
1956
High Society, If Ever I Cease to Love, When I Grow Too Old to Dream, Bye Bye Blackbird, Boogie, Saints, In the Groove, Good Night Irene, Home Sweet Home.

"PAPA" CELESTIN: DIXIELAND KING
Walters (tp), Pierson (tb), J. Thomas (cl), A. French (bj), S. Brown (b), Crosby (p), Louis Barbarin (d).
Imperial
1956
Marie Laveau, Tin Roof Blues, Clarinet Marmalade, Indiana, Tailgate Ramble, March of the Bobcats, World Is Waiting for the Sunrise, Saints, Down by the Riverside, Bill Bailey.

"PAPA" CELESTIN: THE BIRTH OF THE BLUES
Walters (tp), Pierson (tb), J. Thomas (cl), A. French (bj), S. Brown (b), Crosby (p), Louis Barbarin (d).
Imperial
1956
Some of These Days, Dippermouth Blues, Darktown Strutters' Ball, Exactly Like You, Eh La Bas, High Society, Just a Closer Walk with Thee, Birth of the Blues, Bye-Bye Blackbird, Basin Street Blues, Jazz Me Blues, Panama Rag.

OSCAR "PAPA" CELESTIN: NEW ORLEANS JAZZ BAND
Walters (tp), Pierson (tb), J. Thomas (cl), A. French (bj), S. Brown (b), Crosby (p), Louis Barbarin (d).
Imperial
1956

New Orleans, Tiger Rag, Avalon, Didn't He Ramble, Mama Don't Allow, That's a Plenty, Wabash Blues, Slide Frog Slide, Coconut Island, It's You I Love, Anybody Wanna Buy My Cabbage?

HONGO FONGO
The Albert French Band backed up Ernest "Punch" Miller
Miller (tp, voc), W. Eugene (tb), J. Thomas (cl), A. French (bj), F. Fields, Davis (b), J. Kimball (p), Louis Barbarin (d).
Imperial
1962
Milneberg Joys, Alexander's Ragtime Band, Ice Cream, Punch Miller Blues, I Ain't Got Nobody, Hongo Fongo, Back in the Old Days in New Orleans, I've Been Mistreated, Nelly Gray, Somebody Stole My Gal, Shimmy Like My Sister Kate, Lady Be Good.

THE ORIGINAL TUXEDO JASS BAND
Willis (tp), J. Watkins (tb), Frog Joseph (tb), J. Thomas (cl), A. French (bj), F. Fields (b), J. Kimball (p), Louis Barbarin (d).
BASF
1964
Just a Closer Walk with Thee, Didn't He Ramble, World Is Waiting for the Sunrise, Eh! La Bas, Panama, Tin Roof Blues, Original Dixieland One Step.

ALBERT "PAPA" FRENCH AND HIS NEW ORLEANS JAZZ BAND: A NIGHT AT DIXIELAND HALL, VOL. 1
A. Alcorn (tp), W. Eugene (tb), Frog Joseph (tb), J. Thomas (cl), A. French (bj,), Davis (b), J. Kimball (p), Louis Barbarin (d).
Nobility Label
1965
Rampart Street Parade, Way Down Yonder in New Orleans, Marie Laveau, Shine, Darktown Strutters' Ball, Mack the Knife, Alabama Jubilee, St. James Infirmary, Twelfth Street Rag, Savoy Blues, Bourbon Street Parade.

ALBERT "PAPA" FRENCH AND HIS NEW ORLEANS JAZZ BAND: A NIGHT IN DIXIELAND HALL, VOL. 2
A. Alcorn (tp), Frog Joseph (tb), J. Thomas (cl, voc), A. French (bj,), F. Fields (b), J. Kimball (p), Louis Barbarin (d).
Nobility Label

1965
Panama Rag; Angry; Just a Closer Walk with Thee; Mississippi Mud; Yes Sir, That's My Baby; Beale Street Blues; Down by the Riverside; Yellow Dog Blues; Ting A Ling; Didn't He Ramble.

Albert "Papa" French and the Original Tuxedo Jazz Band, Vol. 1
Wilson (tp), H. Eugene (tb), Thomas (cl, voc), A. French (bj, voc), F. Fields (b), J. Kimball (p), B. French (d).
Second Line Label
April 1975
Saints, Marie LaVeau, Mack the Knife, Do You Know What It Means to Miss New Orleans, Basin Street Blues, Go to New Orleans, Just a Closer Walk with Thee, Milneberg Joys, Tailgate Ramble.

Albert "Papa" French at Tradition Hall, Vol. 2
Wilson (tp), H. Eugene (tb), Thomas (cl, voc), A. French (bj, voc), F. Fields (b), J. Kimball (p), B. French (d).
Second Line Label
April 1975
Panama Rag, Jada, High Society, March of the Bob Cats, Twelfth Street Rag, Tin Roof Blues.

The Tuxedo Jazz Band at Tradition Hall, Volume III
W. Brunious (tp), Lonzo (tb), Suhor (cl, sax), F. Fields (b), J. Kimball (p), B. French (d).
Second Line Label
1977
Second Line, Sugar Blues, Petit Fleur, Tishomingo Blues, Sheik of Araby, Five Foot Two, Do You Know What It Means to Miss New Orleans, Bill Bailey, Wabash Blues, Ain't Misbehavin', Wood Chopper's Ball.

Bob French and the Original Storyville Jazz Band
T. Riley (tp), Frog Joseph (tb), Bazoon (cl), E. Marsalis (p), Geo. French (el-b), B. French (d).
Second Line Label
1978
Bill Bailey, Way Down Yonder in New Orleans, High Society, Bourbon Street Parade, Just a Closer Walk with Thee, Saints, Tiger Rag, South Rampart Street Parade, St. James Infirmary.

TRADITION HALL JAZZ BAND
Brunious (tp), Lonzo (tb), Suhor (cl), F. Fields (b), J. Kimball (p), B. French (d, ldr), Geo. French (voc), J. Thomas (voc).
Sandcastle Records
1978
Sleepy Time Down South, Tishomingo Blues, Sensation Rag, Just a Little While to Stay Here, New Orleans, Eh La Bas, Glory Land, Basin Street Blues, Do You Know What It Means to Miss New Orleans, Caravan.

BOB FRENCH'S ORIGINAL TUXEDO JAZZ BAND, FEATURING JORIS DE COCK: 10 JAAR 'T DREUPELKOT
De Cock (tp, voc), Lonzo (tb), Ford (cl, ts), Vappie (contrabass, voc), E. Frank (p), B. French (d, voc).
Tipitina's/ E S Records
1999
Go to New Orleans, Jazz Me Blues, Do You Know What It Means to Miss New Orleans, Down by the Riverside, Rose Room, St. James Infirmary, Sunny Side of the Street, Body and Soul, Night Train, Mahogany Hall Stomp, City of the Million Dreams, Bourbon Street Parade, Ting-A-Ling.

BOB FRENCH'S ORIGINAL TUXEDO JAZZ BAND AND FRIENDS: LIVIN' THE LEGACY
L. Brown (tp, voc), Bartholomew (tp), Lonzo (tb), Maheu (cl), Traub (ts), Huntington (bj, b), Geo. French (b), Severin (b), Torkanowsky (p), D. Crawford (p, voc), P. Longstreth (p), B, French (d, voc), T. Boutté (voc), J. Brooks (voc), E. Charles Jr. (voc).
Royal Tuxedo Records
2000
Milneburg Joys, Muskrat Ramble, Sugar Blues, God Bless the Child, Don't Get Around Much Anymore, What a Wonderful World, Please Don't Talk About Me When I'm Gone, Wabash Blues, New Orleans, You've Got the Right Key but the Wrong Keyhole, St. James Infirmary Blues, High Society.

BOB FRENCH'S ORIGINAL TUXEDO JAZZ BAND & FRIENDS: THE LEGACY LIVES ON
L. Brown (tp, voc), Lonzo (tb), Traub (ts), Maheu (cl), Torkanowsky (p), D. Crawford (p), P. Longstreth (p), Severin (b), Geo. French (b, voc), Huntington (bj), B. French (d), J. Brooks (voc), E. Charles Jr. (voc), T. Boutté (voc), J. Boutté (voc), "Top" (voc).

Royal Tuxedo Records
2000
Bogalusa Strut, Bill Bailey, Crazy, Tin Roof Blues, Whoopin' Blues (Got a
Big Fat Woman), Hello Dolly, I'm Walking, Royal Garden Blues, Georgia
On My Mind, Gloryland, Do You Know What It Means to Miss New
Orleans, Second Line (Joe Avery's Blues).

Bob French's Original Tuxedo Jazz Band
Bartholomew (tp), L. Brown (tp, voc), Lonzo (tb), Maheu (cl), Traub (ts),
Huntington (bj), Geo. French (b, voc), Severin (b), Torkanowsky (p), D.
Crawford (p), B. French (d, voc), J. Brooks (voc), T. Boutté (voc), J. Boutté
(voc), Top (voc).
Cracker Barrel Old Country Store, Heritage Series
2002
Milneburg Joys, Muskrat Ramble, Sugar Blues, Bill Bailey, Royal Garden
Blues, St. James Infirmary Blues, Tin Roof Blues, High Society, Gloryland,
Second Line/Joe Avery's Blues.

Bob French's Original Tuxedo Jazz Band: Three Generations
L. Brown (tp), Payton (tp), Lonzo (tb), Maheu (cl), Vappie (bj), Geo. French
(b), Lemmler (p), B. French (d), Ruffins (voc), K. Longstreth (voc).
Tuxedo Records
2003
Do You Know What It Means to Miss New Orleans, Jada, West End Blues,
Squeeze Me, Last Night on the Back Porch, Creole Love Call, Who's
Sorry Now, Black and Blue, St. Louis Blues, Someday You'll Be Sorry,
Nobody Knows You When You're Down and Out, Dippermouth Blues,
Do You Know What It Means to Miss New Orleans.

Live at New Orleans Jazz Fest 2004
T. Andrews (tp), Brunious (tp, flhrn), C. Johnson III (sop, ts), Severin (b)
Torkanowsky (p), B. French (d), Smith (voc).
Tuxedo Records
2004
Medley: Sleepy Time Down South / Sweet Georgia Brown, Petite Fleur,
Sunny Side of the Street, New Orleans, Halleluiah, Besame Mucho, At
Last, Whoopin' Blues, Royal Garden Blues.

TUXEDO JAZZ BAND AT TRADITION HALL, VOLUME III
Tuxedo Records
2006 re-issue of the 1978 original, remastered as a CD
The content remains the same.

MARSALIS MUSIC HONORS BOB FRENCH
L. Brown (tp), T. Andrews (tb), B. Marsalis (sax), Severin (b), Connick Jr. (p, voc), B. French (d, voc), Smith (voc).
Marsalis Music Honors Series
2007
Bourbon Street Parade, Basin Street Blues, Way Down Yonder in New Orleans, Milneburg Joys, You Are My Sunshine, Burgundy Street Blues, When It's Sleepy Time Down South, Royal Garden Blues, Do You Know What It Means [to Miss New Orleans], Just a Closer Walk with Thee, Saints.

THE ORIGINAL TUXEDO JAZZ BAND CENTENNIAL CONCERT
Baham (tp), Bartholomew (tp, voc), Walker (tb), Dejean (sax), Vappie (bj, voc), Moten (b), P. Longstreth (p), B. French (d, voc), Windsay (voc).
Threadhead Records
2010
Sleepy Time Down South (intro); Sweet Georgia Brown; Exactly Like You; Et Las Bas; Fever; At Last; Darktown Strutters' Ball; Intro/Tenderly; The Monkey Speaks His Mind; Saints; Good Night, Sweet Heart.

GERALD FRENCH AND THE ORIGINAL TUXEDO JAZZ BAND: A TRIBUTE TO BOB FRENCH
Baham (tp), Lucien Barbarin (tb), Fischer (cl), D. Brooks (bj), Moten (b), Sieberth (p), Ger. French (d), Windsay (voc), Solid Harmony (Windsay, Phillips, Chapman) (voc).
11th Commandment Records
2013
Lord, Lord, Sure Been Good to Me; Bogalusa Strut; Dinah; Muskrat Ramble; Darktown Strutters' Ball; Mood Indigo; Basin Street Blues; Do You Know What It Means to Miss New Orleans; Hindustan; Weary Blues; Saints.

Musicians

Musicians who played with the Tuxedo Jazz Band or Brass Band. Birth and death dates. Instrument played with which leader. OC-Celestin, WR-Ridgley, EP-Pierson, AF-Albert French, BF-Bob French, GF-Gerald French, TBB-Tuxedo Brass Band.

MUSICIAN	BIRTH AND DEATH DATES	INSTRUMENT; BANDLEADER
Adams, Placide	Aug. 30, 1929–Mar. 29, 2003	b; OC
Alcorn, Alvin Elmore	Sept. 7, 1912–July 10, 2003	tp; AF
Alcorn, Oliver	Aug. 3, 1910–Mar. 21, 1981	cl, ts; OC
Alcorn, Samuel	1937–July 20, 1998	tp; AF
Alexander, Adolph, Jr., "Tats"	July 15, 1898–Dec. 30, 1969	ct, cl, sax, as, bar-hrn; OC, WR
Alexander, Adolph, Sr., "Old Man," "Taton"	1874–1936	as, bar-hrn; TBB
Alexis, Lester "Duke," "Boots"	Nov. 1, 1914–1990	d; AF
Alexis, Ricard	Oct. 16, 1891–Mar. 15, 1960	cnt, tp, b; OC
Allen, Shamarr	n.d.	tp; BF
Anderson, Andrew	Aug. 10, 1905–Dec. 19, 1982	tp; TBB
Andrews, Troy "Trombone Shorty"	Jan. 2, 1986–	tp; BF
Armstrong, Louis "Pops," "Satchmo"	July 4, 1900–July 6, 1971	cnt; OC
Atkins, Eddie	Oct. 15, 1889 (1887)–1926	tb; OC
Baham, Andrew "Drew," "Da Phessah"	July 22, 1980–	tp; BF
Barbarin, Isidore	Sept. 24, 1872–June 12, 1960	as, mello; BB
Barbarin, Louis	Oct. 24, 1902–May 12, 1997	d; OC, EP, AF
Barbarin, Lucien	Jan. 8, 1905–Mar. 27, 1955	d; OC

MUSICIAN	BIRTH AND DEATH DATES	INSTRUMENT; BANDLEADER
Barbarin, Lucien	July 17, 1956–	tb; BF, GF
Barbarin, Paul, Adolphe Paul	May 5, 1899–Feb. 17, 1969	d; TBB
Barnes, Harrison	Jan. 13, 1889–1960	tb, sax; TBB
Barnes, Paul D. "Polo"	Nov. 22, 1902–April 13, 1981	sax, as, cl; WR
Barrett, Emma "Sweet Emma" "Bell Gal"	Mar. 25, 1897–Jan. 28, 1983	p; OC, WR, AF
Bartholomew, Dave	Dec. 24, 1920–	tp; OC, BF
Bazzle, Germaine	Mar. 28, 1932–	voc; BF
Benson, Hamilton "Hamp"	1885–	tb; TBB
Benton, Tom	c. 1891–c. 1929	gt, bj, man, p, voc; OC
Bocage, Peter Edwin	July 31, 1887–Dec. 3, 1967	vln, cnt, tb, bj; OC, TBB
Bontemps, Willie "Bontin"	c. 1893–1958	bj, g; OC, WR
Boutté, John	Nov. 3, 1958–	voc; BF
Boutté, Tricia "Sista Teedy"	1968–	voc; BF
Braud, Mark	1973–	tp; BF
Brooks, Detroit	1951–	bj, g; BF
Brooks, Juanita	1954–Sept. 9, 2009	voc; BF
Brouchard, Theo T.	n.d.	b; OC

MUSICIAN	BIRTH AND DEATH DATES	INSTRUMENT; BANDLEADER
Brown, Bat	n.d.	cnt; WR
Brown, Leon "Kid Chocolate"	n.d.	tp; BF
Brown, Sidney "Jim Little," "Little Jim"	July 19, 1894–1968	b; OC, EPw
Brunious, Wendell	Oct. 27, 1954–	tp; AF, BF, GF
Cagnolatti, Ernie	April 2, 1911–	tp; OC
Carey, Jack	1889–1934	tb; TBB
Carey, Thomas "Mutt"	Aug. 28, 1891–Sept. 3, 1948	cnt; OC, TBB
Carriere, Sidney "Sid"	n.d.	as, ts, cl; OC
"Cato"	n.d.	b; OC
Cato, Adam	n.d.	p; OC
Celestin, Oscar Phillip "Papa," "Sonny," "Zost," "Dog," "Nostrils"	Jan. 1, 1884–Dec. 15, 1954	tp, leader; 1910-1954
Chapman, Topsy	1947–	voc; BF
Charles, Erving, Jr.	1942–Feb. 26, 2003	b; BF
Charles, Hypolite	April 18, 1891–Nov. 29, 1984	cnt; TBB
Charles, Jesse	June 25, 1900–Aug. 4, 1975	cl, sax; TBB
Clayton, James "Jimmy," "Kid"	Mar. 1, 1901–Dec. 17, 1963	cnt; OC

Musician	Birth and Death Dates	Instrument; Bandleader
Collins, Lee	Oct. 17, 1901–July 3, 1960	tp; TBB, OC
Connick, Harry, Jr., "Boomer"	Sept. 11, 1967–	p; AF, BF
Cornish, William "Willie"	Aug. 1, 1875–Jan. 12, 1942	tb; TBB
Cottrell, Louis Albert, Jr.	Mar. 7, 1911–Mar. 21, 1978	cl, sax; WR, TBB
Cottrell, Louis, Sr.	Dec. 25, 1878–Oct. 17, 1927	d; OC, TBB
Crawford, Davell	Sept. 3, 1975–	p; BF
Crawford, James "Sugar Boy"	Oct. 12, 1934–Sept. 15, 2012	p; BF
Crosby, Octave	June 10, 1898–1972	d, p; OC
Davenport, Wallace Foster	June 30, 1925–Mar. 18, 2004	cnt, tp; TBB, OC, AF
Davis, Humphrey Stewart	1918–July 21, 1985	b; OC, AF
De Cock, Joris	n.d.	tp; BF
DeJean, Allen, Jr.	1980	sax; BF
De Lisle (Deslile), Louis "Big Eye" Nelson, recorded as Louis DeLisle in the 1940s	Jan. 28, 1885–Aug. 20, 1949	tb, cl; 1913 TBB, OC
Derbigny, Arthur	c. 1906–Oct. 20, 1962	sax; WR
Desvigne, Sydney	Sept. 11, 1893–Dec. 2, 1959	ct; TBB
Dodds, Johnny "Dot"	April 12, 1892–Aug. 8, 1940	cl; TBB

Musician	Birth and Death Dates	Instrument; Bandleader
Dodds, Warren "Baby"	Dec. 24, 1894–Feb. 14, 1959	d; OC, TBB
Dolliole, Milford "Stack"	Oct. 23, 1903–May 2, 1994	d; TBB
Dumaine, Louis	1890–1949	ct; TBB
Durand, Maurice	July 4, 1893–Nov. 23, 1961	tp; TBB
Duson (Dusen), Frank "Frankie"	1878–April 1, 1936	tb; TBB
Dutrey (Dutry), Sam, Sr.	1887–1941	cl, sax; TBB, OC
Edwards, Willie	n.d.	tp; TBB
Eugene, Homer Anthony	June 16, 1914–June 7, 1998	tb; TBB, BF
Eugene, Wendell	Oct. 12, 1923–	tb; TBB, OC, AF
Fields, Frank "Dude"	May 2, 1914–Sept. 18, 2005	b; AF, BF
Fields, Mercedes Garman (Gorman) "Candy"	Mar. 1899–Nov. 14, 1967	p; OC
Filhe (aka Fields), George	Nov. 13, 1872–1954	tb; OC
Ford, Clarence	Dec. 3, 1929–Aug. 9, 1994	cl, ts; AF, BF
Foster, Abby (Abbey) "Chinee"	Jan. 9, 1900–Sept. 12, 1962	d; TBB, OC
Foster, George "Pops"	May 18, 1892–Oct. 30, 1969	b; OC
Fouche, Earl	Feb. 5, 1903–n.d.	sax; WR
Frank, Edward	June 14, 1932–Feb. 13, 1997	p; BF

MUSICIAN	BIRTH AND DEATH DATES	INSTRUMENT; BANDLEADER
Frank, Gilbert "Babb"	c. 1870–June 1933	pic; 1910 OC
Franklin, Herman	n.d.	cnt, tp; OC
Frazier, Josiah "Cie"	Feb. 23, 1904–Jan. 10, 1985	d; OC, TBB
French, Albert "Papa"	Nov. 17, 1910–Sept. 28, 1977	bj, g; OC, EP, AF (leader 1958–1977)
French, George	Feb. 23, 1943–	b; BF
French, Gerald "The Giant"	May 9, 1970	d; GF (leader 2011–present)
French, Robert "Bob"	Dec. 27, 1937–Nov. 12, 2012	d; AF, BF (leader 1977–2011)
Garman (Gorman), Mercedes "Candy"—*See Fields, Mercedes*		
Gills, Charles	n.d.	voc; OC
Goldston, Christopher "Black Happy"	Nov. 27, 1894–Mar. 17, 1968	d; TBB, OC
Goudie, Frank "Big Boy"	Sept. 13, 1899–Jan. 9, 1964	ct; OC
Green, Jerome Jerry	June 23, 1910–	tu; TBB
Guerin, Roland	n.d.	b; BF
Hall, Clarence	Feb. 19, 1903–n.d.	cl, as, ts; OC
Hall, Edmond	May 15, 1901–Feb. 11, 1967	cl, sax; OC
Hall, Robert	1899–	ts, cl; WR, OC

MUSICIAN	BIRTH AND DEATH DATES	INSTRUMENT; BANDLEADER
Handy, John "Capt"	June 24, 1900–Jan. 12, 1971	as; OC, TBB
Harris, Joseph Dennis "Joe"	1909–n.d.	as; OC
Henry, Charles "Sonny," "Sunny"	Nov. 17, 1885–Jan. 7, 1960	tb; TBB
Hill, Scott "Scotty"	Oct. 7, 1947–	tb; BF
Holloway, Henry C. "Kildee," "Henri"	1953–	tp, arr; OC
Hooker, George	1882–1929	tu, bar-hrn; TBB
Howard, Avery "Kid"	April 22, 1908–Mar. 28, 1966	tp; TBB
Howard, Joe	1872–1946	cnt, tu; OC, TBB
Humphrey, Percy	Jan. 13, 1905–July 22, 1995	cl, tp; TBB, OC
Humphrey, Willie James, Jr.	Dec. 29, 1900–June 7, 1994	cl; OC
Huntington, William "Bill"	Oct. 2, 1937–	bj; BF
Jackson, Albert "Loochie'"	Mar. 13, 1898–Mar. 3, 1978	tb; TBB
Jackson, Eddie	1867–1938	tu; TBB
Jackson, Henry	n.d.	d; AF
Jefferson, Andrew "Jeff'"	Nov. 24, 1912–July 1, 1985	d; TBB
Jefferson, Thomas	1923–	tp; TBB
Jiles, Albert	Nov. 7, 1905–Sept. 3, 1964	d; OC

MUSICIAN	BIRTH AND DEATH DATES	INSTRUMENT; BANDLEADER
Johnson, Al "Carnival Time"	June 20, 1939–	voc; BF
Johnson, Arthur "Yank"	1878–1938	cnt, tb; TBB
Johnson, Augustus	n.d.	sax; OC
Johnson, "Buddy"	1875–1927	tb; TBB, OC
Johnson, Calvin, Jr.	n.d.	sax; BF
Johnson, Clarence, III	1974–	ts, sop; BF
Johnson, Eddie	n.d.–April 7, 2010	sax; WR
Johnson, Edward "Noon"	Aug. 24, 1903–Sept. 18, 1969	tu, baz; TBB
Johnson, George "Son"	n.d.	as, cl; OC
Johnson, Jimmy	1876–1937	b; WR
Johnson, Joseph "Smoky"	Nov. 14, 1946–	d; AF
Johnson, Tom	n.d.	as; OC
Johnson, Walter "Nooky"	n.d.	ent; OC
Jones, Clifford "Snags"	1900–Jan. 31, 1947	d; OC
Jones, David "Davey"	1888–1956	mello, as, ap-hrn; TBB, WR
Jones, George	n.d.	b; OC
Jones, Leroy	Feb. 20, 1958–	tp; BF, GF

MUSICIAN	BIRTH AND DEATH DATES	INSTRUMENT; BANDLEADER
Jones, Richard "My Knee"	June 13, 1892–Dec. 8, 1945	a-hrn, cnt; OC
Joseph, Ferdinand	n.d.	voc; OC
Joseph, John "Papa"	Nov. 27, 1877–Jan. 22, 1965	b; OC
Joseph, "Squeak"	n.d.	as; OC
Joseph, Waldren "Frog"	Sep. 12, 1918–Sept. 19, 2004	tb; OC, AF
Joseph, Willie "Kaiser"	c. 1892–1951	cl, sax; WR
Julian, Henry	n.d.	sax; TBB
Kelly, Ernest	1886–1927	tb; OC
Kelly, Guy	Nov. 22, 1906–Feb. 24, 1940	ct; OC
Kennedy, Meyer	n.d.	sax, as; OC
Keppard, Louis	Feb. 2, 1888–Feb. 18, 1986	g, tu; TBB
Kimball, Jeanette Salvant	Dec. 18, 1906–Mar. 29, 2001	p; OC, EP, AF
Kimball, Narvin "Henry, Jr."	Mar. 2, 1909–Mar. 17, 2006	bj, b, g; OC, AF
King, Neil	n.d.	b; BF
Klein, Craig	1960–	tb; BF
Knox, Richard	1942–	p; BF
Kohlman, Freddie	Aug. 25, 1918–Sept. 29, 1990	d; TBB

MUSICIAN	BIRTH AND DEATH DATES	INSTRUMENT; BANDLEADER
Landry, Alcide "Al," "Big"	1880–1949	ct; TBB
Lawrence, Joseph Addison	n.d.	voc, ent; OC
Lee, Sam	n.d.	ts; OC
Lemmler, Matthew "Matt"	1967–	p; BF
Lenares (Lenois), Ezab "Zeb"	c. 1885–c. 1928	cl; TBB, OC
Lewis, George (legal name was George Louis Francois Zenon. His mother spelled the last name as Zeno.)	July 13, 1900–Dec. 31, 1968	cl; OC
Lewis, Robert "Son Fewclothes"	Mar. 10, 1900–June 24, 1965	d; TBB
Lewis, Walter, Jr.	1915–June 10, 2002	p, voc; OC
Lindsay, Johnny	Aug. 23, 1894–July 3, 1950	tb, b; OC
Longstreth, Kimberly	July 1974–	voc; BF
Longstreth, Paul	Oct. 1971–	p; BF
Lonzo, Frederick, "Freddie"	Aug. 20, 1950–	tb; BF
Love, Charles Edwin "Charlie"	Oct. 6, 1885–Aug. 7, 1963	cnt; TBB
Madison, Louis "Kid Shots"	Feb. 19, 1899–Sept. 1948	tp; TBB, OC, WR, OC
Maheu, Jack	1930–	cl; BF
Manetta, Manuel "Horse," "Fess"	Oct. 3, 1889–Oct. 10, 1969	all instruments; OC

Musician	Birth and Death Dates	Instrument; Bandleader
Marrero, John	1895–1945	bj; OC
Marrero, Simon	1897–1935	tu, b; OC
Marsalis, Branford	Aug. 26, 1960–	sax; BF
Marsalis, Ellis	Nov. 14, 1934–	el-p; BF
Martin (Martyn), Henry	1895–1932	d; TBB
Matthews, Nathaniel "Bebe"	1890–May 27, 1961	d; TBB, WR
Matthews, Ramos "Brown Happy"	1886–Oct. 20, 1958	d; TBB
Matthews, William "Bill"	May 9, 1889–June 3, 1964	d, tb; OC, WR, OC
McClean, Richard	Jan. 25, 1898–c. 1968	b, bj, g; OC
McCullum (McCullough), George, Jr.	1906–1938	tp; TBB, WR, OC
McDermott, Thomas "Tom"	1957–	p; BF
Metoyer, Arnold	1880–1935	tp; TBB, WR
Mitchell, Leonard	n.d.	g; bj; OC
Morgan, Andrew	Mar. 19, 1903–Sept. 19, 1972	cl, sax; TBB
Mosley, Baptiste "Bat"	Dec. 22, 1893–Aug. 28, 1965	d; TBB
Mosley, Edgar	Nov. 12, 1895–Oct. 1962	d; TBB
Moten, Richard	Nov. 5, 1952–	b; BF, GF

MUSICIAN	BIRTH AND DEATH DATES	INSTRUMENT; BANDLEADER
Mukes, "Little Jim," "Groundhog"	n.d.	d; TBB
Nelson, Louis "Big Eye"—See De Lisle, Louis Nelson		
Nelson, Louis	Sept. 17, 1902–April 5, 1990	tb; OC
Noone, Jimmy	April 23, 1895–April 19, 1944	cl; TBB, OC
Ogden, Dave Robert "Bob"	c. 1888–Mar. 18, 1963	d; OC
Oliver, Joseph "Joe," "King"	May 11, 1885–April 8, 1938	ct; fill in for OC
Oxley, Dave	May 1, 1910–July 20, 1974	d; OC, AF
Palao, James A. "Jimmy" aka Jimmy Spriggs	c. 1880–1928 or 1935	vin, sax, a-hrn; TBB, OC
Palmer, Roy	1892–1964	tb; TBB
Patterson, John	n.d.	ts; OC
Paul, Emanuel "Manuel"	Feb. 2, 1904–May 23, 1988	ts; TBB, OC
Paulin, Ernest "Doc"	June 22, 1907–Nov. 20, 2007	tp; OC
Payant (Payen), Joe	1875–1932	as; TBB
Payton, Nicholas	Sept. 26, 1973	tp; BF
Perez, Manuel	Dec. 28, 1871–1946	cnt; TBB
Petit, Buddy, born Joseph Crawford	c. 1880–July 4, 1931	cnt; TBB, fill in for OC

Musician	Birth and Death Dates	Instrument; Bandleader
Phillips, Joylynda	1973–	voc; BF, GF
Picou, Alphonse Floristan	Oct. 19, 1878–Feb. 4, 1961	cl; TBB, OC
Pierce, Joseph De La Croix (Lacroix) "Dee Dee"	Feb. 18, 1904–Nov. 23, 1973	tp; TBB
Pierson, Earl	n.d.	ts, as, sop, cl; OC
Pierson, Edward "Red," "Eddie"	Aug. 1, 1904–Dec. 17, 1958	tb; OC, EP, leader; 1954–58
Piron, Armand A.J.	Aug. 16, 1888–Feb. 17, 1943	vln; Piron/Williams Band 1916
Player, Mitchell	1970–	b; BF
Pork Chops—*See Smith, Jerome*		
Porter, John	1890–Nov. 2, 1958	bar-hrn, tu, souse; TBB, OC
Prejeaud (Pajeaud), Willie	1895–May 12, 1960	ct; TBB
Pulphus, David	1973–	b; BF
Reason, Lionel	c. 1909–	p; OC
Ridgley, William "Bebe"	Jan. 15, 1882–May 28, 1961	tb; TBB, OC, WR.
Riley, Amos	1879–1925	tp; WR, fill in for OC
Riley, Theodore "Teddy"	May 10, 1924–Nov. 14, 1992	tp; BF
Rivers, James	n.d.	sax, fl, bgp; BF
Robichaux, Joseph "Joe"	Mar. 8, 1900–Jan. 17, 1965	p; OC

MUSICIAN	BIRTH AND DEATH DATES	INSTRUMENT; BANDLEADER
Robinson, Nathan "Big Jim"	Dec. 25, 1892–May 4, 1976	tb; TBB
Roseby, Raz "Butch"	n.d.	tb; OC
Rouson (Rouzon), Joe	n.d.	sax ; OC
Rousseau, August	1894–1956	tb; TBB, OC
Ruffins, Kermit	Dec. 19, 1964	tp, voc; BF
Russ, Henry	Aug. 7, 1903–	cnt; OC
Saguaro, Sam	n.d.	tu; OC
Sanders, Frederick "Fred"	1971–	p; BF
Santiago, Lester "Blackie"	Aug. 14, 1909–Jan. 18, 1965	p; OC
Sayles (Sales), Emmanual Emanuel	Jan. 31, 1907–Oct. 5, 1986	bj, g; WR, BF
Scott, Alex "Rock"	c. 1895–c. 1943	sax, b; WR, OC
Severin, Chris	1958–	b; BF
Sieberth, Larry	Nov. 5, 1953–	p; BF, GF
Sims, George	1872–	bar-hrn; TBB
Singleton, Arthur James "Zutty"	May 14, 1898–July 14, 1975	d; TBB
Smith, Ellen "Big Fine"	1967–	voc; BF
Smith, Jerome "Pork Chop"	Dec. 26, 1895–	ent; OC

Musician	Birth and Death Dates	Instrument; Bandleader
St. Cyr, Johnny	April 17, 1890–June 17, 1966	bj, g; OC
Suhor, Donald J. "Don"	Aug. 30, 1932–Jan. 27, 2003	cl, sax; BF
Tervalon, Clement	Nov. 13, 1915–	tu; TBB
Thomas, Blanche	Oct. 16, 1922–April 21, 1977	voc; AF
Thomas, Joseph "Brother Cornbread"	Dec. 3, 1902–Feb. 18, 1981	cl; OC, EP, AF, BF
Thornton, Cecil	n.d.	sax; WR, OC
Thoumy, Willard	n.d.	cl; OC
Tio, Lorenzo, Jr	April 21, 1890–Dec. 1, 1933	cl; OC, TBB
Tio, Lorenzo, Sr.	c. 1865–c. 1920	cl; TBB
Tio, Luis "Papa"	c. 1863–1927	cl; TBB, OC
"Top"	n.d.	voc; BF
Torkanowsky, David "Tork"	1956–	p; BF
Traub, Eric	1947–	ts; BF
Trepagnier (Trippania), Ernest "Ninesse"	1890–April 11, 1968	d; TBB, OC
Vappie, Don	1956–	bj, contrabass, voc; BF
Venet, Seva	1969–	g; BF
Veret (Verrett), Harrison	Feb. 27, 1907 or 1909–Oct. 18, 1965	bj, g; OC

MUSICIAN	BIRTH AND DEATH DATES	INSTRUMENT; BANDLEADER
Walker, Strephen "Steve"	1975–	tb; BF
Walters, Albert Fernandez	July 19, 1905–	tp; AF
Washington, Isidore "Tuts," "Papa Yellow"	Jan. 24, 1907–Aug. 5, 1984	p; OC
Watanabe, Mari	1964–	p; BF
Watkins, Joseph	n.d.	tb; AF
Watson, Joseph "Joe"	c. 1895–c. 1926	cl; TBB, WR
White, Amos	Nov. 6, 1889–July 2, 1980	ct; fill in for OC, OC
Williams, Alfred	Sept. 1, 1900–April 30, 1963	d; TBB
Williams, "Black Benny"	c. 1890–July 6, 1924	d; TBB
Williams, Clarence	Oct. or Nov. 8, 1898–Nov. 6, 1965	p, voc; OC
Willigan, Bill	n.d.	sax; OC
Willigan, Jim	c. 1902–c. 1930	d; OC
Willis, Joshua F. "Jack"	April 15, 1920–n.d.	tp; AF
Wilson, Clive	1942–	cnt; AF
Windsay, Yolanda	1964–	voc; BF, GF
Young, Gilbert	n.d.	tp; WR
Zeno, Henry	c. 1885–c. 1918	d; TBB, OC

Bibliography

Abbott, Lynn. "Remembering Mr. E. Belafield Spriggins: First Man of Jazzology." *78 Quarterly* 1, no. 10.

Arnold, Abagail. Interview by David Hillyer. May 4, 1958. Hogan Jazz Archive (HJA), Tulane University.

Barnes, Paul. Interview by Jane Hillyer. March 13, 1971. HJA, Tulane University.

————. Interview by Richard B. Allen, Lars Edegran and Barry Martin. June 16, 1969. HJA, Tulane University.

Bocage, Peter. Interview by Barry Martin. February 6, 1962. HJA, Tulane University.

Breckenridge, Esther Dupuy. Interview by David Hillyer. May 4, 1958. HJA, Tulane University.

Bushell, Garvin. *Jazz From the Beginning*. Ann Arbor: University of Michigan Press, 1991 (org. pub. 1988).

Carrole, Leigh, III. Interview by David Hillyer. May 4, 1958. HJA, Tulane University.

Celestin, Oscar "Papa." Interview by John Curran and Edward Hebert. May 8, 1953. HJA, Tulane University.

Charters, Samuel B. *Jazz New Orleans 1885–1963: An Index to the Negro Musicians of New Orleans*. Rev. ed. New York: Oak Publications, 1963 (org. pub. 1958).

Cottrell, Louis. Interview by Bill Russell. Aug. 1, 1961. HJA, Tulane University.

Curran, John G. Interview by David Hillyer. May 13, 1958. HJA, Tulane University.

Dead Rock Stars Club. http://thedeadrockstarsclub.com.

Dufour, Charles L. Interview by David Hillyer. May 4, 1958. HJA, Tulane University.

Dupuy, Homer. Interview by David Hillyer. May 4, 1958. HJA, Tulane University.

Foster, Abby "Chinee." Interview by Bill Russell. March 9, 1961. HJA, Tulane University.

———. Interview by Bill Russell and Ken Grayson Mills. June 29, 1960. HJA, Tulane University.

———. Interview by Bill Russell and Ralph Collins. March 16, 17, 18, 19 and 21, 1960. HJA, Tulane University.

Foster, "Pops." *The Autobiography of Pops Foster New Orleans Jazzman: As Told to Tom Stoddard*. San Francisco: Backbeat Books, 2005.

Frazier, Cie. Interview by Barry Martyn, Bill Russell. January 9 and 18 and February 2 and 16, 1961. HJA, Tulane University.

———. Interview by Lars Edegran and Jane Julian. January 19, 1972. HJA, Tulane University.

———. Interview by Ralph Collins and Bill Russell. December 14, 1960. HJA, Tulane University.

Gambit New Orleans News and Entertainment. http://m. bestofneworleans.com/gyrobase/new-orleans-know-it-all.

Goldston, Christopher. Interview by Richard Allen and Bill Russell. January 13, 1959. HJA, Tulane University.

————. Interview by Richard Allen and Marjorie Zander. April 11, 1962. HJA, Tulane University.

Guide to New Orleans and Louisiana Music. http://www.satchmo.com.

Gushee, Lawrence. *Pioneers of Jazz: The Story of the Creole Band.* New York: Oxford University Press, 2005.

Hasse, John Edward. *Jazz: The First Century.* New York: Harper Collins, 2000.

"A History of Opera in New Orleans." http://neworleansopera.org/a-history-of-opera-in-new-orleans.

Hogan Jazz Archive, Tulane University. http://jazz.tulane.edu. Premier New Orleans jazz history resource.

Huber, Leonard V. *New Orleans: A Pictorial History.* Gretna: Pelican Publishing, 1991 (orig. pub. 1971. Crown Publishing).

Hurricane Brass Band. http://www.hurricanebrassband.nl/index.htm.

Jazz and R&B Landmarks of Dowtown New Orleans. http://webpages. charter.net/davidmmiller/neworleans.htm.

Kerrigan, Elizabeth O'Kelly. Interview by David Hillyer. May 4, 1958. HJA, Tulane University.

Kerrigan, Jack. Interview by David Hillyer. May 4, 1958. HJA, Tulane University.

Kimball, Jeanette Salvant. Interview by Bill Russell. February 10, 1962. HJA, Tulane University.

Kimball, Narvin. Interview by Bill Russell. November 15, 1961. HJA, Tulane University.

Leslie, James. "Papa's Horn of Plenty." In *Jazz 1958: The Metronome Jazz Year Book*. Edited by Bill Coss. New York: Metronome Company, 1958.

Lord, Tom. *The Jazz Discography*. New York: Cadence Jazz Books, 1992.

Manetta, Manuel. Interview by Bill Russell. July 1 and August 26, 1958. HJA, Tulane University.

———. Interview by Nesuhi Erlegun, Bob Campbell, Bill Russell and Richard Allen. March 21 and 28, 1957. HJA, Tulane University.

Matthews, William "Bill." Interview by Bill Russell. March 10, 1959. HJA, Tulane University.

McCaffrey, Kevin. *The Incomplete Year-by-Year, Selectively Quirky, Prime Facts Edition of the History of the New Orleans Jazz and Heritage Festival*. New Orleans: e/Prime Publications, 2005.

Moyer, Evelyn Sinclaire. Interview by David Hillyer. May 4, 1958. HJA, Tulane University.

Moyer, Marietta M. Interview by David Hillyer. May 4, 1958. HJA, Tulane University.

National Park Service. http://www.nps.gov.

New Orleans Jazz. http://www.nojazz.org.

O'Kelly, Mary Lucy Hamill. Interview by David Hillyer. May 4, 1958. HJA, Tulane University.

Raben, Erik. *Jazz Records: 1942–50 Discography*. Copenhagen: Stainless/ Winter Moon.

Raeburn, Bruce Boyd. 2002. "Duck and Blow: A Brief Overview of Black Musicians' Unions in New Orleans." HJA, Tulane University.

————. *New Orleans Style and the Writing of American Jazz History*. Ann Arbor: University of Michigan Press, 2009.

Ramsey, Frederic, Jr., and Charles Edward Smith. *JazzMen*. Reprint. New York: Harcourt, Brace, 1967 (orig. pub. 1959).

Renaudin, William. Interview by David Hillyer. May 4, 1958. HJA, Tulane University.

Ridgley, William. Interview by Bill Russell and Ralph Collins. June 6, 1959. HJA, Tulane University.

————. Interview by Richard Allen. April 7, 1961. HJA, Tulane University.

————. Interview by Richard Allen and Marjorie Zander. April 11, 1961. HJA, Tulane University.

Rose, Al. *Storyville, New Orleans: Being an Authentic, Illustrated Account of the Notorious Red-Light District*. 3rd paperback ed. University: University of Alabama Press, 1982 (orig. pub. 1974).

Rose, Al, and Edmond Souchon. *New Orleans Jazz: A Family Album*. Rev. ed. Baton Rouge: Louisiana State University Press, 1978 (orig. pub. 1967).

Rust, Brian. *Jazz Records A–Z 1897–1942*. Rev. ed. London: Storyville Publications & Co., 1972 (orig. pub. 1970).

Schuller, Gunther. *Early Jazz: Its Roots and Musical Development*. Reprint. New York: Oxford University Press, 1986 (orig. pub. 1968).

Soards New Orleans City Directory. 1926. New Orleans: Soards Directory Co.

Stokes, W. Royal. *The Jazz Scene: An Informal History from New Orleans to 1990*. New York: Oxford University Press, 1991.

Teachout, Terry. *Pops*. New York: Houghton Mifflin Harcourt, 2009.

Ulanov, Barry. *A History of Jazz in America*. New York: Viking Press, 1952.

University of Chicago Press. http://www.press.uchicago.edu.

White, Amos. Interview by Bill Russell. Aug. 23, 1958. HJA, Tulane University.

Williams, Martin. *Jazz Master of New Orleans*. New York: Macmillan, 1967.

Index

Z

About the Author

Sally Newhart has lived in Pennsylvania, New York, Massachusetts and Louisiana. She likes the music and gardening here in New Orleans and plans to stay.

Courtesy of Freddie "Blue" Goodrich, Freddie Blue Works Photography.

Visit us at
www.historypress.net

· ·

This title is also available as an e-book.